"In this profoundly erudite and eloquent book is a startling ancient secret that will forever alter the way we think about the origins of western civilization."

— PIR ZIA INAYAT KHAN

"Peter Kingsley is more than a master storyteller. He is a magician who reveals the golden thread of truth which makes its way through time and space, secretly holding the fabric of our world together. *A Story Waiting to Pierce You* reveals the surprisingly mystical origins, and purpose, of western culture as well as what it means to participate in its eternal unfolding right now."

— ADYASHANTI

"This is a book of miracles—deceptively simple, actively profound. It is a core story of human becoming, the secret history that holds the codes to what we were and what we yet may be."

— JEAN HOUSTON, author of *A Mythic Life* and *The Hero and the Goddess*

"A blazingly alive work of scholarship and spiritual insight"

— JACOB NEEDLEMAN, author of *What is God?* and *The Heart of Philosophy*

"*A Story Waiting to Pierce You* is, simply, piercing. Peter Kingsley is a master of adamantine prose and peerless scholarship. His work is truly worthy of that overworked term *wisdom*. And he is a master stylist: he turns you upside down and inside out without your knowing it is happening. This book will inspire, delight and enlighten many but will also challenge others because it is a mirror that reflects our most stubborn prejudices about the origins of our most sacrosanct cultural beliefs. And for that, Peter Kingsley deserves the highest praise."

— LARRY DOSSEY, M.D., author of *Reinventing Medicine* and *The Power of Premonitions*

# A Story Waiting to Pierce You

# A Story Waiting to Pierce You

## to Pierce You

### MONGOLIA, TIBET AND
### THE DESTINY OF THE WESTERN WORLD

PETER KINGSLEY

First published in the United States in 2010 by
The Golden Sufi Center
P.O. Box 456
Point Reyes, California 94956.
www.goldensufi.org

Fourth (revised) printing, 2018.

Kingsley, Peter.
    A story waiting to pierce you : Mongolia, Tibet, and the destiny
of the Western world / by Peter Kingsley.
        p. cm.
    Includes bibliographical references.
    ISBN 978-1-890350-20-8 (hardcover : alk. paper) —
ISBN 978-1-890350-21-5 (pbk. : alk. paper)
    1. Pythagoras. 2. Abaris, the Hyperborean. 3. Shamanism—
Mongolia—Influence. 4. Shamanism—China—Tibet—Influence.
5. East and West. I. Title.
    B244.R3K56 2010
    182'.2--dc22
                                    2010014402


Hardcover ISBN 13: 978-1-890350-20-8
Paperback ISBN 13: 978-1-890350-21-5

# CONTENTS

❖

Foreword by Joseph Rael  xi

1. The Aim  1

2. The Journey  17

3. The Goal  33

4. The View  51

5. The Endless Joy  67

Notes  87

And now what's going to become of us without
the barbarians? Those people—
they could have offered some kind of solution,
might have been our unbinding

*Konstantinos Kavafis*
*Alexandria, Egypt, 1898*

The last stages are here now. The Purifiers are coming

*Thomas Banyacya*
*Third Hopi Mesa, Arizona, 1986*[1]

# Foreword

MY SPIRITUAL NAME is Beautiful Painted Arrow in the language of North Central New Mexico Picuris Pueblo Indians. It is pronounced Tslew–teh–koyeh (flight of the rainbow people leaving their mark as they travel into a double rainbow connecting mother earth and father sky).

I feel honored to write this introduction for an elder brother, Peter Kingsley. *A Story Waiting to Pierce You* is a story for us all.

I was not able to read this book. It was impossible to read as I usually would, silently to myself. Instead of reading it I had to sing it out loud, because this book is a magnificent song. It is not just a masterpiece, written by a master of English prose. It is a true *encanto*, an incantation. Its rhythm is beautiful, amazingly beautiful—its cadence fantastic. Most books are pretty boring, just facts and information. But this book is pure music. It sings to the reader.

This is the real thing. In each paragraph of the book, the Spirit is there. This is what the native people of the Americas have been trying to say, but were never permitted to. This song is the song of wisdom that we native people have not been allowed to sing. This book is not just Peter Kingsley's wisdom. It is their wisdom, our wisdom. And it needs to be spoken, to be sung and heard again for the sake of the young ones. Because he does what needs to be done and says what has to be heard, I consider Peter Kingsley to be one of the most courageous people on the planet at this moment.

When making a careful study and review of this book I suddenly realized that he is teaching us about the reality of the ancient mysteries reaching from our past into the present moment. Because he is an interpreter of mysteries I began to read those mysteries as beings and vibrations and, as I began to read, they slowly and gently came out of the pages saying "Thank you for rediscovering us, it is so good to be home!" I heard voices as though from a far away place. The mysteries came, nine of them, and I wrote them as they appeared inside my senses:

one — **Hyperborea** — arm of awareness, moving straight as an arrow, leaving as it travels sparks of delight, a radiance for eyes to see, a sun giving placement to a pure clarity.

two — **Abaris, skywalker** — creator of trails made of wisdom, to follow to find heavenly streams of light.

three — **Avars** — to come from the heavens to wash the night time moons.

four — **In a circle** planting new universes.

five — **Phurbas** — flutterings of feathers in the direction of awakening those who still sleep.

six — **Gold** — where divine beauty is enshrined full of knowing.

seven — **Mongols** — bringers of goodness to the people of all the directions.

eight — **Tulkus** — crystallized essences of carrying, lying on planet earth covered only by a blanket of sky.

nine — **Hermotimus** — caretaker of perceptions, of reflections, of imaginations.

I do not use the number ten, because the reader should be the one to add the tenth step.

Soon life will no longer be as it was: life will return to breath, matter and movement and then it will return bringing a new creation.

This book is a gift for our time. Thank you, Peter Kingsley, for all of us.

Joseph Rael, Beautiful Painted Arrow
Marvel, Colorado

# 1

# The Aim

I T WAS almost as if he appeared out of nowhere, holding the mysterious object in his hand.

But they had a name for the place he came from. Hyperborea, to Greeks living near the Mediterranean over twenty-five hundred years ago, was the beyond of the beyond. It was the land that lay to the furthest north or far, far east on the other side of the frozen mountains from where the bitter winter winds will blow.

To get there was simple. You walk until you reach the limit of your ability and there is no way you could possibly go any further.

Then you start walking. It was a world of perfect contradiction: the land that dreams are made of but that no ordinary human would even dream of thinking to go.

This is the place Abaris appeared from. Or at least that was how he came to be called.

And just the same as with other remarkable people who seemed half human, half something else as they moved among the Greeks, he also had a nickname he was known by. His was Skywalker.

But there is something I almost forgot.

When Abaris Skywalker arrived he was traveling in a trance. As he went around Greece he walked in a state of ecstasy, holding a god inside him—the god Apollo.

No one knows any more quite what to do about Abaris.

Of course there have been the experts who are quick to dismiss him as completely unreal: as nothing but an ancient fantasy or mythical phantom not even worth a second thought. And then there are those who have agreed there must be something more to him than that. They argue that he clearly has the makings and the markings of a shaman—of one of those strange, uncontrollable healers and mystics found across the world but especially familiar in the areas around Siberia and Central Asia.

As for where he came from, though, and why and how: it appears nobody knows.

Hardly a word is written or spoken about him nowadays. But when there is such an all-embracing silence this is not always because there is nothing to be said.

Sometimes it can be because to look too closely would mean starting to see things that fall outside the frames of our understanding. After all, history—our history—is not so much a matter of what is remembered or repeated as of the things we prefer to leave unsaid.

So I will take a deep breath and move straight into saying a bit about Abaris Skywalker. His mystery is an easy one to solve. But it leaves behind a far greater one: the mystery of our own past, of the history we have forgotten, of who we are.

Abaris cut a striking figure as he arrived, foreigner from a mythical land.

But he was not the only strange person who, at around the same time, happened to be traveling in a state of trance either out from the northeastern edges of Greece towards the home of the Hyperboreans or back in the opposite direction towards Greece.

They, too, were ecstatic servants of Apollo. And with these other figures you can tell their itinerary more clearly than in the case of Abaris.

After leaving Europe and everything familiar far behind, eventually they came to the region of the Altai Mountains in Central Asia. And the other side of those mountains—beyond the gateway of Central Asia which opens out onto the vastness now known to us as eastern Siberia and Mongolia, as China and Tibet—was Hyperborea, Abaris' home.[2]

That brings us to the word itself, Abaris.

People's names can often tell us a great deal about them. And Abaris is not a Greek name at all. On the contrary, the only other times you will ever find it mentioned in the Greek language it always happens to be used as the name for a mysterious group of people whose origins disappear into the past but who first came to be talked and written about by their ancient neighbors: the Chinese.

Today they are known as the Avars. And this is precisely what, in Greek, the name Abaris meant: "the Avar."

As for the Avars' ancestral home, the source of their culture and their traditions and skills: it was Mongolia.[3]

That leaves us with one more detail—Abaris' nickname.

A long time ago in a world very different from our own, before the word Skywalker had become so familiar because of the film industry and thanks to popular influence from the mythology of Tibet, this very same name was well known in two countries.

One was Tibet; the other was Mongolia.

And aside from being a standard way of describing someone with magic powers beyond anything human, in those regions it had a second sense as well.

"Skywalker" also meant an arrow.[4]

When Abaris came he was carrying an arrow in his hand.

Or at least it looked like an arrow. One of our Greek sources uses a word to describe it that could apply just as well to any sharp missile or dart; another says the object was unusually bulky. And then there is the tradition that mentions something so strange no one could blame so many scholars for silently leaving it aside.

It says Abaris' arrow was metallic—or to be more precise, was made of gold.

But the fact is that, even if this had been the most perfectly ordinary arrow, Greeks would still have had a hard time finding some sound reason for why he was carrying it around in his hand.

Certainly they tried. Any justification for the unfamiliar will always seem better than none. And just as surely they failed, because the truth is there was nothing they could say that was going to explain Abaris' behavior away. People close to the Mediterranean were not in the habit of holding an arrow wherever they went.[5]

So the Greeks are not much help; but we are a little more fortunate than them. We already know where to look.

Avars were perhaps the most skilled and effective archers the world has ever seen. Without their arrows and bows they would never even have begun making their way west out of Mongolia and, centuries after Abaris, almost bringing Byzantium to its knees.

Where they came from, the science and art of archery were something so intricate we can hardly start to grasp it any more. And for Mongols, unlike Greeks, even the bow was second in importance to the arrow. Every particular detail in the process of making arrows or using them demanded absolute attention. Each single stage of selecting the material, crafting the shaft and tip and feathers, shaping the arrow, creating, painting, finishing it, called for extraordinary care.

The distances they could be shot, their accuracy, were legendary. And then there is the sound.

Different arrows were designed to produce different noises as they flew through the air. There were arrows to imitate the cries of different animals, to draw birds out of hiding by mimicking the calls of their mates or the shrieks of their young, to scare all kinds of creatures so they would leave the safety of their hiding places and run from the protection of their lairs, to freeze the stags in their tracks.

And during war arrows became the core of a precisely premeditated system. Before battle, in different phases of the battle, different arrows making different sounds were shot by different leaders and commanders to signal an entire variety of instructions and commands.

Of course there was also the element of fear. Avars knew better than anybody how to terrify their enemies through sound, how to root them to the spot and stop them even starting to run away. The whistle and piping of arrows in flight were war's petrifying harmony—its exquisitely orchestrated symphony of death.

To hold an arrow was to hold the fate of many people in one's hand. So there is nothing surprising in how, for Avars as well as other Mongols, it was the arrow that became their supreme symbol of power. To carry an arrow while alive was to hold a tangible token of authority, plain proof of identity, the most visible sign of mission or rank. And when the great ones died they were honored by having arrows respectfully buried by their side.[6]

Life, together with death, were both encoded in the arrow. And inside this whole symbolic code one specific detail still stands out.

The famous institution of the great Khan—spiritual and political leader to his people—became enormously influential as it swept from Mongolia across Central Asia into India, Persia, eastern Europe. If we trace it back as far as we can to its source we are brought, once again, to the Avars. And originally, when the great Khan sent out a messenger or ambassador as his official representative and envoy, he gave him a particular token to carry with him so everyone would recognize the carrier's mission and rank. The same tradition was preserved unchanged for centuries not only among Mongols, but also in Tibet.

That token was an arrow made of gold.

And this may be the best time to mention something else I came close to the edge of forgetting.

Reports by Greeks about Abaris are quite clear that he was much more than just some casual visitor or tourist when he happened to reach their country. In fact they say exactly what we already might have expected to hear.

They say Abaris arrived on a special mission as ambassador to Greece from the people of Hyperborea—as their official representative and envoy.[7]

And if it seems we are near the end of this story, the truth is we have only just begun.

Nothing would be easier in our modern, splintered, fragmented world than to suppose Abaris must have arrived as ambassador with his arrow on a simple diplomatic mission so he could play some purely political role.

But what happened in those days was different from the ways things are done now. And as a matter of fact the ancient sources are very clear about the real purpose behind his coming so far.

They say he was sent to the land of the Greeks as a healer. Or to be a bit more precise: they state, quite plainly, that he arrived as a purifier and prophet to bring back balance to the earth and offer each place he visited protection from the plague.

In other words, when Abaris headed for the West he was coming as a shaman.

And so we are led back once again to his people, the Avars. In that part of the world they considered their ancestral home, it was normal for nomadic tribes to be particularly proud of their primordial ability to keep the places they arrived at protected from plagues.

As for why they felt this, the reason is easy to understand. It was because they saw themselves, since the dawn of time, as a people of shamans.

Shamanic tradition was the cover they slept under every night, the ground they walked above each day. It was their strength and protection. When Avars fought, they won not just through knowledge of weaponry but through magic; were so hard to resist because they were masters of shamanic warfare.[8]

And their chief symbol, the arrow, was never just some physical object.

It was alive. In the eyes of Mongols arrows have always been a magic weapon: the chief seat of shamanic power. And some arrows, especially ones made of silver or gold or stored in a metal quiver, are far more potent than any others. Legends describe how—endowed through incantations with the unfailing power to find their way—they are able to clear a passage straight past insurmountable obstacles, right over impassable landscapes, as they follow their own undeviating path through the air by effortlessly steering and guiding themselves.

But, above all, the arrow is an instrument allowing shamans to enter a state of ecstasy: for taking them

11

straight into another world. In that state of ecstasy things become quite clear which are hidden from ordinary eyes. And here lies the problem if you want to approach what a shaman is or does from outside, because then you will see nothing but all the superficial forms you are already familiar with reflected right back to you.[9]

This is the tragedy of trying to understand with the mind what needs a different organ of understanding. And if only historians of the western world could see what longs to be seen, if they had just paid attention where attention is due, they would have saved themselves so much pointless fighting about Abaris.

For centuries scholars have claimed there are two irreconcilable accounts of his arrival in the West. Then they battle with each other to the point of silent exhaustion over which of these two ancient Greek accounts is correct. One is the tradition that says Abaris was carrying his arrow. The other says that the arrow was carrying Abaris —finding its own path for him, guiding him without ever deviating or failing, clearing a passage for him past every obstacle and across insurmountable landscapes, steering him on his way around the earth with as little effort as if it was lifting him right through the air.

But they are both correct.

The two accounts are not contradictory at all. On the contrary: they are simply different aspects of one intricate, original tradition just like the opposite sides of a single coin.

As to how its two sides belong together, there is no need to look too far for our answer. All we have to remember is one basic shamanic principle—that those who carry an object of power in their hand are carried by it. Abaris holds the arrow so it can take him wherever he needs to go.[10]

To us this may sound very strange, but only because we have learned to forget that the way things appear to us outwardly is often the exact opposite of a deeper truth. And in the case of Abaris nothing could be more natural, or more urgently necessary, than this intimate connection between his arrow and him. The man has been taken by a state of ecstasy: is absorbed in a different world. It should be obvious to anybody that, with his attention fixed on another reality and without something in this one to hold or guide him, he would be utterly lost before his journey even began.

Now we can understand why, for Tibetans, the word "skywalker" means both an arrow and a shaman.

The point here is not just that shamans move as swiftly, and easily, as arrows but that only with the help of their arrow are they able to move at all. Without the power of an arrow the shaman can do nothing because an arrow is the symbol of what a shaman must become.

And here, too, is the reason why Tibetans use this very same word for referring to someone immersed in a state of ecstasy.

In that state, the tip of an arrow becomes the point of one's whole existence. The intense focus demanded of an arrowmaker, unable even for a moment to turn away to the right or left, is also the one-pointedness essential for shooting an arrow at its mark—and is the same single-pointedness needed for seeing straight through appearances into a reality where everything is one.

There you are the shaper and shooter of yourself, the target and the goal. Everything begins as it ends in that moment, outside of time, when the arrow is shot straight into your heart and penetrates the whole of your being.

And there, where the shaman becomes nothing, is the magical point from which all good things come. [11]

# 2

# The Journey

A MBASSADOR from the beyond, purifier, walker through the sky, Abaris came to be many things to many people.

But, above all, he left his mark on the Greeks with that arrow he carried in his hand. Thanks to it he won his reputation as overcomer of obstacles, the great remover of obstructions. He also became famous as the master of incantations who with the help of his arrow was able to chase away diseases and epidemics and control the weather by taking command of all the winds which, while left unchecked, were devastating the people and their land.

And Greeks were stunned by his habit of talking to the arrow as if it was a person. There is no way they could have known that even down to modern times it has been the practice of Mongol shamans to discuss things with their arrow, speak to it as if talking to a living being, give it instructions, ask its help with the task in hand.[12]

But apart from the mysteries of his golden arrow, and aside from the strangeness of his incantatory abilities, there is one enigma about Abaris which in a way is more of a riddle than anything else.

This is the simple fact that he managed to walk such phenomenal distances.

And what makes such a feat all the more mysterious, what makes historians even less inclined to take the figure of Abaris seriously, is the detail about him traveling in an ecstasy or trance. Distances so huge would be hard enough to cover for anybody walking normally in a sober frame of mind, let alone for someone in another state of consciousness.

But there is a forgotten possibility here, waiting so silently to be seen: a possibility people never even stop to look at because it would turn everything upside down.

This is that Abaris' trance might just have been the one crucial factor which allowed him, holding his god inside him, to travel so far—and that those accounts about him flying through the air on some magical arrow or dart are simply a hint as to the very particular way in which he walked.

And even after he arrived in Greece he walked, and walked.

They say the only places he would ever stop to stay were inside the sacred sites and temples he came to. No one saw him eating or drinking out in the open. And of course people living near the temples he came to, close to the places where he healed, always made a great deal of his visit: somehow managed to imagine their own region or city was unique, so absolutely special.

But when we stand back a bit and watch the picture of his movements from a distance, then a striking pattern begins to emerge. As some ancient Greek writers were careful to point out: Abaris was not the kind of person who just wandered here or there.

Instead, he walked around the land "in a circle."

That, from our western point of view, might sound like nothing. But, as so often, what sounds like nothing can be a clue to making sense of the whole if we only take the time to learn its language.

And in fact this is yet another of those riddles we are lucky enough to be able to solve far easier than any Greeks could ever manage—thanks to the descriptions, so dutifully preserved for us by Chinese observers, of traditional Mongol customs.

All we have to do if we want to start understanding why Abaris, Avar envoy from Hyperborea, carried his arrow in a circle is to take note of the official title given by the Mongols to their envoys. They called them the "arrow-circulators," their "arrow-circulating representatives," because of the way they would walk as fast as they humanly could while only stopping when they had to—carrying their arrow in a circle around the land.[13]

And, if you choose, we can stop our story here; count up the riddles solved, call it a day, close the book.

Or we can go on following the circlings of Abaris towards what matters most.

❖

There is something I never quite had a chance to say about the Avars.

This is that their all-important arrows had a very particular shape. Each of them was triple-bladed—with three raised edges running the whole way from the shaft right down to the tip.

And nothing could be less accidental than the fact that over time this same, identical design would become incorporated into one of the most powerful magical objects ever known to Tibetans or Mongols.

The *phurba* has always had its central place in the sacred history of Tibetan Buddhism. But even though Buddhists were very quick to make this ritual weapon their own, its origin is neither Buddhist nor Indian. It comes, just like the triple-bladed arrowhead itself, from the shamanic traditions of Mongolia and Central Asia.

All sorts of materials have been used for creating and shaping phurbas. It goes almost without saying that far more crucial than choosing some perfect substance is the nature of the attention put into making them.

But by and large they tend to be metallic. And over the centuries they often have been made of gold.

To look at them you would think they are just what they appear to be: a sharp-pointed dart or ornamented spike. But, as invariably is the case with shamans and their objects, appearances are deceiving.

Through the whole of its history the phurba has had one constant secret—the fact that this magic weapon, this extraordinary embodiment of shamanic power, works by striking from a distance. It will ruthlessly find its goal, pin down, control, overcome and even destroy by traveling with its user's consciousness through space.

This is why its blade has the shape of an ancient arrowhead. This also is the reason why phurbas and arrows are so easily interchangeable from a ritual point of view. And this is why, in spite of their extra bulkiness and weight, a standard name for phurbas is "little arrows."

For a shaman to become a shaman means learning how to ride these metal arrows, just like Abaris, in the air—especially when the aim is to heal and purify by fighting with the spirits of sickness and striking them down.

And here is the reason why, in the eyes of Tibetans and Mongols, the phurba has such a unique reputation as overcomer of obstacles: as the greatest remover of obstructions. The most famous shamans are the ones who allow themselves, with the help of incantations, to be carried by their phurbas through the air so they can chase away diseases and epidemics and plagues and change the weather by taking control of those spirits behind the winds which otherwise would continue devastating people and the land.

But the traditions about flying phurbas are even stranger than that.

Always perfectly true to its nature, the phurba made its way into the heart of Tibetan Buddhism by traveling through the air. According to legend the most treasured example of all, the archetype of every single phurba in existence, arrived at the monastery where it would be protected and honored for centuries by simply flying there. At the same time each year it had to be carried, ever so carefully wrapped, to the Dalai Lama himself at the Potala palace in Lhasa to bless the land as well as the people—and to stop it from flying away.

The phurba will never let itself be tied down by religious differences or disputes between Buddhists and shamans. They owe their power to it, not the other way around. And as one modern shaman of Mongol ancestry has been willing to explain, this ritualistic arrow is not just the essential instrument for healing and for prophecy.

It also is needed for flying straight through this world into another reality.

He then goes on to say that the only real way to hold a phurba, or be carried by it, is by becoming it—to the magical point where you and the phurba are one. [14]

And now is the time to bring all this talk about flying back down to earth.

Long ago, before trains or trucks or planes, people in Tibet and Mongolia had a little problem. Deserts were immense, mountains gigantic. And to travel from place to place, especially for sacred purposes, could seem to take forever.

So to get around they learned to fly.

It was quite simple. We in the West have all our small ideas about possibilities, impossibilities; and until the time we die they may even seem to make some sense. But this is only because we have forgotten what human beings are capable of. We learn to squeeze the greater part of our lives into making a bit of money or making a mess of the earth, and can do a wonderful job of them both. But the dim awareness buried inside everybody of those other potentials is what terrifies us at night, makes us so dissatisfied each day.

For Mongols and Tibetans the key lay in discipline. Above all it was a matter of patience—a few hard years of total focus on discovering how to breathe in certain ways and, with the help of silently repeated incantations, control the element of air until the body becomes almost weightless.

At first, the goal is just the opposite of what you might think.

The point would be to become quite still. That was because the creators of these methods understood how the starting-point of utter stillness leads to the mastery of unbelievable speed. It was the same essential paradox well known, in ancient Greece, to the servants and priests of Apollo: that the secret to all movement lies hidden in the mystery of what never moves.

And for Tibetans or Mongols this practice of stillness led to the freedom of being able to move with the winds, of being able to travel further and faster than any human can imagine.

Their wind walkers could go anywhere; cover enormous distances with apparently effortless ease; find their way over every conceivable obstacle and straight past the most impassable landscapes as if flying through the air.

But they were only able to do any of this on one single condition.

As long as they were walking they had to stay in an unbroken trance, holding their god inside them. That single-pointed focus, just like the intense attention required of an arrowmaker or demanded of someone shooting arrows at their mark, had to be kept totally undisturbed. If anything or anybody disrupted it, the divine presence which had been guiding them would be gone in an instant—and could shake their body so badly the shock would be deadly.

Now we can understand why Abaris was never seen stopping to eat or drink. Nothing could be allowed to interfere with the concentration of these walkers through the sky or break their extraordinary awareness as they moved across our world, this strange world of separation and distance, while living in another.

And just as Apollo's ecstatic servants were famous for their utterly impersonal expression of otherworldly calm, these travelers' constant state of consciousness showed through in the completely expressionless calm on their faces—while they walked and walked supported by the phurba they were carrying in their hand.

In fact we still have vivid descriptions of how, even though these walkers were the ones holding their metallic arrow, to anyone watching closely it would look just like the phurba was holding them. [15]

Walking this way was an important convenience for people needing to reach a teacher, lead a ritual, take part in sacred ceremonies at a distance.

And it performed another crucial role. It could also be a sacred ritual in itself.

The initial training for Tibetans lasted three years and months and days. Then the real training would begin. It continued for around eleven more years. And by the end of that process the person had become nameless, any traces of individual identity left behind.

Most of the preparation took place in isolation, darkness, stillness. And finally the chosen representatives, confirmed by oracles and other authorities, would be approved to do their work—the work of walking the land for the sake of purifying it.

Each of them is only allowed to eat or drink just a little at night, in private, while taking a short break from the walking. Then they are on their way again: purifiers offering protection to every place they come to.

Just like Abaris they walked from sacred site to sacred site, temple to temple, looking to neither left nor right. At one point on their journey they would arrive in Lhasa where all the doors of the Potala palace were thrown open for them so they could rush from room to room, purifying through their simple attention wherever they went, before being ushered into the presence of the Dalai Lama himself.

Then, without so much as a single word crossing anyone's lips, they have moved on—walking in a great circle around the land.[16]

And it takes such sensitivity, so much discipline, so much patience, even to start grasping the peculiar irony and humor of the situation we are faced with. After all, we have come to a strange turn of events in the West where only by looking to Tibet and Mongolia are we able to understand ancient Greek texts ignored or distorted by the best of experts for thousands of years.

There is no need to look very far for an explanation of all the mystery surrounding Abaris and his identity, his place of origin, his purpose.

Or rather: we just have to look much further than most people are even willing to dare. Every indicator and pointer and hint we could possibly need is there, ready to be noticed. And what they reveal should be enough to take anybody's breath away.

They show the total focus of a Mongol shaman come, at the dawn of western culture, to help purify the land of the Greeks—arriving by a path that allows us to trace the most esoteric of practices right from the heart of Tibetan and Mongol Buddhism into the heart of our western world.

The resulting picture is an absurdity, an unthinkable impossibility, and an absolute necessity. For a long time there has not been the slightest doubt that many of the most striking traditions in Tibetan Buddhism reach far into the distant history of pre-Buddhist Mongolia or Tibet. And to anybody willing simply to pay attention to the facts it has been obvious that the ritualistic phurba goes all the way back to the metallic arrows of the Mongols: back to a time when outer and inner worlds still functioned together, when there was no split between spiritual or military warfare, between sacred or profane, and when even ambassadors and envoys were still carriers of magical powers.

But to draw the easy conclusion that these aspects of Tibetan or Mongol Buddhism had many centuries of history behind them is one thing.[17] To be able to trace them back for thousands of years, right to the beginnings of western civilization, is quite another.

That turns nearly everything—our histories of the West, as well as Tibet and Mongolia too—on its head.

Sent by the god Apollo with an arrow in his hand, Abaris carried a thread of one-pointedness joining the East to the West. And the thread is so fine it has nearly gone unseen.

But it also is so strong, so strangely unbreakable, that this arrow tells a story far too significant for us to forget.

# 3

# The Goal

A ND THEN he gave it away.

You may well have had trouble guessing how this story is going to come to an end. In fact nothing could seem more abrupt, more absurdly disruptive, than that all of a sudden he should give up the one object so important to him on his journey.

The truth is, though, that the future rarely unfolds as our minds predicted. Reality is far more than some simple set of rules about what to do or the way to do it.

And with people like this, who live in service not to our flimsy expectations but to the power of life itself, the unexpected is just to be expected.

They say Abaris arrived from Hyperborea carrying the arrow, taken by it, healing with it—then placed it in the hand of one particular person.

His name was Pythagoras: the same extraordinary philosopher who played such a crucial role in seeding our western culture, in laying the foundations for this whole world we think we know.

But that handing over of the arrow was not some random act of abandonment.

We are told he gave it to Pythagoras as a special gesture of mutual trust, of the secret understanding between them. And from Abaris' point of view this, to us, unexpected turn of events makes absolute sense. It happened to be an ancient Mongol custom for envoys or leaders traveling through foreign regions to leave the arrow they had taken on their journey in someone else's hand—as a very particular gesture of the mutual trust or secret understanding between them.

And in the case of people coming from a country, a culture, as strongly traditional as Mongolia such a custom will tend to last a long while. Over two thousand years after the time of Abaris, on his own way out to the western edges of his lands to meet a man who soon would become famous as the first person to receive the title of Dalai Lama, the great Mongol ruler Altan Khan would still make sure he placed an arrow in the hand of the one local governor he felt safe entrusting with his possessions.

In this intricate code of graceful behavior, to offer up the arrow was far more than just a gesture of trust.

It also was a sign, not of weakness but of generosity in strength.

And the arrows themselves, as tangible tokens of importance and rank, very clearly map out the transfer of authority from person to person.

They are the plainest and most visible proofs not only of a willingness, but above all of the ability, to empower.[18]

Of course most western writers are quite clueless about any of this—living in a world of their own creation with no real sense for those debts they still owe to something so vast, so seemingly different from themselves.

That detail they found in their sources about the Hyperborean Abaris handing his arrow to Pythagoras has something transparently authentic about it. At the same time it lies right on the furthest edges of what westerners have been willing or able to grasp.

And the lengths they went to just so they could drag it inside their own familiar sphere of understanding, of unsophistication, are a crying shame.

Oblivious to every subtle shade of refinement in Mongol etiquette, soon people were trying to decide if Abaris had submissively surrendered his arrow or Pythagoras had simply snatched it away from him instead. And we can so easily see all the sad stages of that tragedy they helped to create—making Abaris Skywalker appear a feeble-minded foreigner in need of some good Greek education, reducing him to little more than a docile and subservient old man.

Above all, this was a tragedy of misplaced piety on the part of Pythagoras' well-intentioned disciples: a perfect lesson in the dangers of devotion. They jumped at any chance to assume that the best way to honor and idealize one's teacher is to exalt him to the purest heavens while demeaning or undermining everyone else, even an apparent stranger who had been far more intimate with their own teacher than they could ever hope to be.

But it was a tragedy jointly produced by others, too.

There used to be a group of Athenian thinkers who in their arrogance imagined they were legitimate heirs of Pythagoras themselves. They were well aware of how dependent Greeks had been on the supposedly barbarian East: that was much too obvious to ignore. Even so, in their inventiveness they cultivated one particular theory which was to have a devastating destiny.

This was the theory, so reassuring, so satisfying to their vanity, that whatever the Greeks inherited from the East they would automatically improve on and always— thanks to their natural superiority—take to some greater height.

So what had been, with Abaris and Pythagoras, in perfect alignment became tilted. Gestures of respect began being treated with the most distressing disrespect, the delicacies of etiquette all wiped away. Proofs of mutual understanding were almost immediately misunderstood and replaced with nothing but demonstrations of special-ness: of petty exclusivity.[19]

All of a sudden symbols of oneness had become twisted into our familiar myths of supremacy and separa-tion. And it was this illusion of superiority, that mirage of knowing better, which now has brought us to the end of our world.

In his ecstasy he knew what he would find before even arriving.

That could sound quite surprising; but this is the way things go. Most people are just dragged through their lives in spite of themselves, grabbing at anything to hold on to, guessing at some sense to everything unfolding all around them, always left without a clue.

And meanwhile the real events, the true changes, are the ones brought about in a state of ecstasy by those who see and know.

As for Abaris, this is what he was allowed to see in advance. He had been shown by the god Apollo—his guide alive inside him—that in Pythagoras he would find a living incarnation of Apollo.

This was the secret at the heart of their mutual un-derstanding, was the source of the trust between them both, was the reason behind Abaris handing over the arrow he had been carrying so long: his ability to identify a great being who, out of compassion for others, decided to become embodied by taking birth in human form.

And this all makes such strangely perfect sense when we stop to consider the origin of those ideas about incarnation, and reincarnation, that start appearing in the West with figures like Pythagoras.

People have wondered for hundreds of years if such mysterious ideas were invented in Greece or might have arrived instead from somewhere else, for instance India. And after so much time one single thing can clearly be said for sure, which is that in origin these ideas are not Greek at all.

On the contrary: they came from far away in the East.

But even so, no generalization in the world can possibly soften the blow of noticing who plays the crucial role of recognizing Pythagoras for who he was and winning his intimate trust.

Just one single individual is named in the ancient literature as being able to do this. And he was not some Pythagorean disciple. Neither is he even a Greek. Neither, for that matter, was he Indian.

He is a Mongol.

And now there are all those other little details that so effortlessly, so simply, start falling into place. To mention only one example, our fullest account of the meeting between them explains how Abaris managed to identify

Pythagoras so precisely. It says he was able to recognize him as a divine incarnation "both from the noble marks he observed in him and from the proofs of identity revealed to him in advance."

Western interpreters are as quick to skip over this passage as they can be, even if at the cost of mistranslating it. And there is no reason not to do so, because it really means next to nothing from a western point of view.

But the moment we change our perspective these same words, preserved in ancient Greek, instantly come alive. As a matter of fact they happen to be the perfect description of something so strikingly unique it perhaps has become the single most popular characteristic of Tibetan and Mongol Buddhism.

What this Greek text describes is the routine formalities among Tibetans, as well as Mongols, for identifying a great being who out of compassion has decided to become embodied by taking birth in human form.

And one very famous word exists for referring to such a living incarnation. The word is *tulku*.[20]

This was not the end of the strangenesses.

There is something staggeringly significant about the simple fact that the first person in the West ever mentioned for identifying a divine incarnation was a Mongol. That he managed to recognize him according to standard procedures laid down in later Mongol traditions, that he acknowledged him with the Mongol gesture of handing over an arrow: this is just, in its strangely unexpected way, to be expected.

But all these details placed side by side still only make up a small part of the picture, because there is something else about that meeting between Abaris and Pythagoras waiting to be said. And it has nothing to do with either Pythagoras or Abaris as human beings.

Instead, it has to do with what brought the two of them together—the god Apollo.

Often Apollo is referred to as the most perfectly Greek of all the Greek gods: as embodying the finest and purest ideal, the quintessential character, of ancient Greek culture.

And there is a certain truth to this which no one could deny. But you will only be able to find that truth when you have come to realize we know as little about the original nature of western culture as we do about Apollo.

By the weirdest of alchemies he has been transformed into the supreme representative of reason, sheer clarity shining out in the brightest light of day. This is the kind of trick our minds sometimes like to play with history— the sort of extravagant romantic fantasy it can be such a temptation to fall for, of projecting our own imaginings and needs onto the realities of another world.

The fact far too few people are yet willing to face is that, above all, he was a god of ecstasy: of the unearthly stillness found in another state of consciousness, in the ground of prophecy where every part of life is known as one.

To be sure, he was a god of light. But that light of his is a brightness we have no experience of any more.

In reality he was a god of plague and purification; of healing and utter destruction, so terrifyingly ruthless he could scare the living daylights out of every Greek divinity he went near; of people speaking the strangest of languages; of bows sending arrows that come when least expected, always arriving from far away. And far from loving some easy clarity he was a god of impossible enigmas, buried like brilliant sparks in an unbearable darkness where normally no one would dare to look; of songs and poems bound up as magic incantations; of riddles wrapped inside a mystery that, understood, will tear you apart.

But as for being so quintessentially Greek, this is the greatest deception of all. It was something Greeks already forced themselves to believe with the same intensity as madmen trying to cling on to sanity by the skin of their teeth. And on the surface it could even seem believable.

There was just one problem, though.

This is the fact that their myths and legends told a totally different story—the story of how Apollo, the god they thought they knew, happened to have the most mysterious and timeless of ties with Hyperborea.

Even before his appearance the ties are there. He was said to have been born by his mother after she came down from Hyperborea to Greece in the form of a wolf, accompanied by wolves. Ancient and modern writers have battled to make sense of the story, which is so easy to understand when we bear one little detail in mind: the legends of Mongols as well as other Central Asian people about how originally they had been born from a wolf in the most remote and sacred regions of their land.

And there are the other traditions handed down by Greeks—traditions that describe how it was Hyperboreans who in the dawn of history came to their country and, back when gods still walked with humans, had founded the oldest Greek shrines for Apollo at the heart and navel of the earth. From then on Apollo was almost impatient, always waiting, ready to leave Greece for the land of the Hyperboreans as often as he could while the Greeks would do everything they could to keep him with them.

It was one of western culture's most impossible paradoxes that this being they so depended on was so stubbornly unwilling to be pinned down: that this god they so much needed to be theirs never could be. You can still feel the strain and tension of people struggling to convince themselves as well as him that this perfect insider, this complete outsider, belonged with them.

To assume he must feel more at home with Hyperboreans than in Greece—nothing could seem more natural. But, at the same time, to spell it out in too much detail would be a virtual taboo.

To admit he might prefer to think of himself as more Hyperborean than Greek: that could seem perfectly logical.

But, for the Greeks themselves, it would have been a confession of utter defeat.

And now we can start to grasp a little better how extraordinary that meeting between Abaris and Pythagoras happened to be.

For Pythagoras to agree with Abaris that he was an incarnation of the great god Apollo: from the Greek point of view this is already enough of a shock to explain why the teaching center he had so carefully created in Italy would soon be burned down by enemies and destroyed.

But this was not the only thing he is described as admitting to his visitor—that stranger who had walked so far from Hyperborea. Pythagoras also took one other, unthinkable step of making an announcement which first would be repeated in the local area and soon spread through the rest of Greece.

He announced not just that he, himself, was Apollo. He said he was Hyperborean Apollo.

45

And in putting these two words together he produced an enigma of unimaginable dimensions. With that simple little statement he ripped aside the veil of Greek supremacy; created a tear in the fabric of isolation which later Greeks would work so desperately to repair.

But what to us already seems more than enough is, for people like him, always only the start. And that, too, was just the beginning—because what Pythagoras was actually doing, with this riddle of his which strips every trace of normal sense away, was making a tear in the fabric of the mind.

He was saying that even though Apollo might appear to be the most Greek of all Greek gods, really he belonged somewhere else in the beyond of the beyond. And he was saying that although he, Pythagoras, might look just like a Greek man in a Greek body his real being had come all the way from Hyperborea.

To our minds that feed on separation and distance this is sheer nonsense. But, even so, in the middle of such ridiculous unclarity at least he kept one thing perfectly clear—which is that Abaris was not alone in making the long journey from Hyperborea to Greece.

Apollo had come with him. And every step of that coming spoke of a purposeful intelligence we can hardly conceive of any more.

First Abaris had made all the necessary preparations. He quite literally cleared the ground for the god who guided him as he walked in his sacred circle—cleansing, purifying, realigning the elements, bringing what had become confused and chaotic back into focus.

And, for his part, Pythagoras had incarnated as a Greek in the West. Soon he would become famous as a culture–creator, a shaper of civilization, as originator of the word "philosophy" so he could give some name and sound to the sacred activity of searching for a wisdom that will change every human being who dares go near it and transform any civilization willing to embrace it.

But such a great gesture of generating a new culture for a sacred purpose, such a divinely compassionate initiative for the sake of a human race that has lost its way, can never be performed by a single person alone. Someone else was needed, somebody from outside, to help along the process by activating and confirming him in his role.

So when everything was ready and where it ought to be, when Abaris already had brought the land back into balance and there was an inner harmony in the air, he completed what had been started by handing over the arrow and empowering Pythagoras to do the work he was born to do.

In his own body, in a spirit of perfect openness and blending, Abaris made possible the transmission from East to West. It needed someone to come out of the East, and plant this seed of the West, by inserting into the ordinary world of humans the fertilizing power of the divine.

This is the mysterious dance in which germs of new cultures are scattered and sown. And this is the secret of that mutual understanding and trust between Abaris and Pythagoras—Apollo trusting and understanding Apollo, two bodies but only one being, like recognizing like.[21]

# 4

# The View

THERE WAS someone even closer to Pythagoras, if such a thing is possible, than Abaris.

I should warn you that to come near such nearness is to approach a reality where whatever we are familiar with will all start to melt away. There is simply nowhere else to go, though, if we are to bring to an end this story begun so long ago.

His name was Hermotimus and his home was Clazomenae—a small city right on the western edge of Asia where the ancient web of trade routes stretching all the way from China arrives at the Mediterranean Sea.

But to someone like him our ordinary concepts of geography, our conventional methods of measuring and assessing, mean very little. What he succeeded in doing stayed almost hidden, while if you were to look to him for some obvious form of accomplishment you would be utterly disappointed.

And this is just how he wanted it, and still does.

He became famous for lying down lifeless on the ground where he lived. Then, his body as still as if it were dead, he traveled in his consciousness wherever he was guided to go. And when the ecstasy was over, after he started standing up, he would share with those around him the things he had been shown—a messenger bringing news of whatever he managed to hear and see.

He has, to say the least, posed quite a puzzle for anyone trying to understand him. The stream of names created to describe who Hermotimus was has flowed thick and fast. Some historians like to call him an ancient Greek shaman; others give him titles not nearly as nice. And the end result of so many decorative labels has been to push him out of sight as far as he will go.

The trouble is, as I am sure you will have noticed, that the more we push puzzles away the bigger they tend to grow and grow. And if only it were possible to dismiss Hermotimus as just some isolated creature, an exotic freak of nature all alone on the outermost fringes of the known world, we might almost be able to say the puzzle has been solved.

But he was much more than that—because it was out of him, from Hermotimus' inner experiences in a state of ecstasy, that every western theory about the nature of conscious awareness originally grew.

Thinkers thought about what consciousness is, then thought even harder, then taught the coldness of their own uncertainties. Hopelessly unaware that the source of human thinking can never be grasped by thinking they started playing their great guessing game, first in

Hermotimus' own home town of Clazomenae and then at Athens and Alexandria and Rome.

But the impetus behind so much thoughtful fascination with the nature of consciousness was not some speculative theorist. On the contrary, it happened to be an ecstatic who was an expert at separating his conscious awareness from his human body at will.[22]

And this is the way it always is. At the origin of every guess stands someone who knows.

There is something else, too, about Hermotimus.

He happened to be nearer than anybody, even Abaris, to Pythagoras because he and Pythagoras were one and the same being. Each of them was viewed as just another reincarnation, as simply a different physical manifestation appearing at the appropriate time in the identical line of Hyperborean Apollo.

And among the very few reports preserved about him is an account of how, hundreds of years before the man Pythagoras was born, it came to be his turn to prove his own identity to the Greeks around him. We are told that he went a little way down the west coast of Asia to the great local temple of Apollo where, to everyone's amazement, he demonstrated who he was by picking out and correctly identifying a possession of his in his previous incarnation.

Of course nobody in the West was going to leave such an odd tradition alone for long. And sure enough, there was plenty of trouble from Greeks and Romans waiting for it around the corner.

Early Christian fathers were horrified by what it so clearly implied: the existence of a continuous spiritual lineage even older than theirs. To discredit it they cooked up as many kinds of contemptuous abuse as they were capable of, used every ounce of virulence and mockery they could muster. And scholars since then have hardly had the will to handle it any better, or start digging it out from under the rubble of misunderstandings that covered it over.

But no more is needed than the most fleeting familiarity with eastern customs to recognize, without any trouble, the routine procedure adopted by Tibetan or Mongol tulkus for proving who they are—by correctly picking out the objects that used to belong to them in their previous incarnation.

The logic behind all of this, the precision and consistency, are impeccable. Hermotimus was acting perfectly true to form as one in the line of reincarnations that later would come to be identified by a Mongol ambassador from Hyperborea, using Mongol techniques, as embodiments of an Apollo who belonged where the Mongol himself had just arrived from: Hyperborea.

There are no flukes here, no accidents, any more than with Pythagoras or Abaris. But this time the conclusions are far more terrifying than before, because they plunge us centuries past Pythagoras towards the oldest recorded history of the Greeks.

In the face of such a logic every other logic begins to crumble; the hardest and fastest distinctions start fading away. And the irony is that there never was any need for things to happen this way.

All along it would have been so much easier if we had just managed to remember those infinitely enigmatic accounts left behind by early western historians about how the most sacred Greek shrines had been founded by the same strange visitors from Hyperborea who, accompanied by Apollo himself, once brought the Greeks their most precious and primordial traditions.[23]

And here we are a few thousand years on, oblivious to the givers, the gifts all forgotten.

Even so, you would be wrong to suppose forgetfulness is a purely western disease. In fact there is no way it could ever be confined to West, or East, because among the most important things we have forgotten is that East and West are one.

You may well ask how it can be that practices lying right at the roots of our own, western civilization are only familiar to us now through popular films about Tibetan mountains or beautifully robed Buddhist monks. The question is an excellent one, because nothing could seem more ridiculous: more inexplicable.

But really this is not so hard to understand. And the reason for such a peculiar state of affairs is that tulkus are no longer just living incarnations of compassionate wisdom.

They also have become the quintessential embodiment of Tibetan Buddhism in all its absolute, its total, uniqueness. Or so we are supposed to believe.

The exotic reality of reincarnating tulkus is associated in our minds almost exclusively with the dazzling mystery of the Dalai Lama. But in the history of Tibet, even Buddhist Tibet, the Dalai Lamas are only a recent phenomenon. And much further back in time, towards the remotest origins of Tibetan Buddhism, lies something else: something we can comment on, notice the effects of, but which in itself will always remain a secret wrapped inside layers of silence.

Right at its dawn, its mythical beginnings, the introducers of the new religion used the power of the ancient shamans to overcome the shamans; to destroy them, pin them down. Far from simply being importers of some Indian wisdom, they were shown how to use the shamans' magic to take away their magic—by taking over their traditions, renaming them, making them their own.

And the shamans themselves were given a choice. Forget or convert; run or die.

This is how the story began and is how it would continue, century after century. And when eventually a Tibetan monk managed to make his way out to the lands of the Mongols in 1578, after months of trudging, he would end up digging the ancient pattern even deeper. The formalities of his meeting, on June 19$^{th}$, with the great ruler known as Altan Khan were framed by an almost perfect symmetry. The monk gave Altan Khan a special, honorary title. And in exchange he became the first Tibetan to receive the Mongolian title "Dalai Lama." Altan Khan acknowledged the Dalai Lama as a tulku, and the Dalai Lama recognized Altan Khan as a tulku too—as the reincarnation of Kublai Khan, belonging in an unbroken line extending back to Genghis Khan himself.

The great Khan asked some special favors of a religious nature. And in return the new Dalai Lama asked one particular favor of the Khan. This was that he wipe out every single trace of shamanism among his Mongol people, smash and burn their sacred instruments, exterminate their practices, silence their songs, and annihilate any shaman stupid enough to resist.

Soon, with the assistance of Mongol troops sometimes lining the streets to keep order in Lhasa, the Dalai Lamas had become rulers over a whole country. With their newfound power they could easily afford to be generous by offering support to Naqshbandi Sufis who arrived at Lhasa from Central Asia asking for help in their struggles against other Naqshbandi Sufis; but closer to home most people were a little less fortunate. And over the centuries, across Mongolia as well as Tibet, orders for extending the persecution and extermination of shamans were not just issued with the new rulers' silent approval.

On the contrary, the instructions came straight from the Dalai Lamas' own mouths and hands—along with the practice of revising the past, rewriting history, modifying the course of events that already had taken place.

And now in these very different times the sincerest messages of kindness and nonviolence, of spiritual oneness and global peace, are almost enough to let it all fall away: to erase any remaining memories of those forced conversions, mass murders, communities and traditions destroyed, of people's land being seized from them together with anything else they could name until they no longer remembered who or what they were, and of the silenced songs that if they ever happen to be heard still have the power to take your heart away.

But even so, in spite of everything, we still can manage to trace back step by step the origins of the famous tulku institution to where it really comes from: back, beyond Buddhism's dramatic appearance on the stage, to the ancient shamanic practices of Tibet and Central Asia.

Of course, nowadays, wherever you look you will find hardly a word said about any of this. But the reason for such silence is not any lack of solid evidence—evidence still accessible in the annals of the old Tibetan kings or in the records of the first Buddhist tulkus ever to leave their mark across Tibet and among the Mongols, along the Silk Road, around the great deserts of the Tarim Basin stretching up above Tibet towards the Altai Mountains.

Quite to the contrary: it simply is due to the spell of forgetfulness cast over the whole matter so many hundreds of years ago.[24]

❖

And now is the time for a completely different kind of magic.

This is the kind that will let us remember rather than forget: is what will allow us to piece back together all the parts of ourselves scattered between East and West. But the irony is, we have forgotten even what it means to remember.

Really to remember is not to hold on to the details and trappings of how things used to be, to get caught by our attachments or aversions to the past. Whatever has been done is over, was done as well as it could be.

Remembering is simply a matter of recollecting the essence of ourselves—of gathering our own finest pollen into the present for the sake of the future.

Times change; are always slipping, shifting. Things that once were necessary, allowable, are not even possible any more because the energies and opportunities are no longer the same. Suddenly the directions of life have switched and a new path opens up for us ahead: full of obstacles to begin with but easier and easier for anyone to follow as soon as the first travelers have cleared the way. Before we know it, yesterday's impossibility will be tomorrow's laziness.

And this particular way ahead offers more, asks for more. It means being able to look much further into the distance than before—not just ahead, but to the left and right and also behind. For that to happen, though, we have to be able to let go of all our little countries and religions and timespans until even Tibet or the Mediterranean are only specks on a map; until even a spread of three thousand years is just child's play.

Very little exists in the history of Buddhism that can take us back even close to the time of Abaris or Pythagoras or Hermotimus. But there is something else that can: the earth with its seas and dry land, the two-legged creatures wandering its surface together with the strange words they tend to speak, and the generous surprises it always is so happy to provide.

And this time the surprises arrive from the West instead of the East—although not from the West as Europe. They come from the West as America, where west of west turns out to be east of east.

The careful respect for rebirth as a fact of life, for people going through the process of proving who they are by picking out the objects that used to belong to them in their previous incarnation: we come across these practices not just in Tibet, or Mongolia, or at the western tip of Asia with Hermotimus, but also somewhere else.

Up until a while ago they silently continued in the far northwestern corner of the Americas—or, to be a little more precise, in particular among the northern tribes of British Columbia. Sometimes, miraculously resisting the Christian attempts at extinguishing them, they still do.

And just like so many other details in this story, the fact that they are known here rather than anywhere else is not some accident or isolated fluke. On the contrary, it happens to be just one small part of a far vaster pattern.

This is the pattern that, thousands of years before the Greeks appeared on the scene, started forming with the waves of migration from what now is Mongolia and Siberia across to the Americas. And the situation it gave rise to is something we westerners—for all our cultivation—have never even started to grasp.

We tend to believe that reincarnation is the discovery and uniquely intellectual property of India, aside from the occasional brief brush of contact with the Greeks. But this is nothing more than one little fragment in the grand fantasy invented by the so-called "higher" cultures to preserve their sense of superiority and self-importance.

In reality all of this is just a dream, alongside our other dreams about how indigenous shamanic cultures are not as ethical as us or not able to share our special access to a transcendent reality behind the world of the senses. And of course they are illusions we are quite entitled to hold on to, until the flowers and leaves start falling off our culture and we are drawn back into the soil each of us comes from.

But one thing we can be perfectly sure of is that life will never serve us in our search for some lasting sense of superiority. Life is oneness. It gives, then takes; has no liking for special consideration. And with those who are most neglected, rejected, abused: there is where the greatest reality always lies hidden.

Long before the dawn of our civilized dreaming, reincarnation was already a teaching embedded in the shamanic cultures of what now is known as Mongolia and Siberia and Central Asia. And, if we look, we can still see the beauty of the shape made by Mongol shamans as they learned to fly—opening their wings to the right and left, spreading them to the east and west.

One wing is what took them across the Pacific to the Americas. And the other, along with an Avar who in the West would come to be remembered as Abaris Skywalker, is what carried them across western Asia to the Mediterranean.

As for those ocher-robed Tibetan monks who have done such a wonderful job of faithfully preserving the ancient tulku tradition through the centuries: they were only its protectors, after all, not its inventors. And they might just fall over in a faint if they were to realize that, when they so tragically were forced out of Tibet in the twentieth century, they were not the first to bring it to the West.

On the contrary, it already had been brought to Europe right at the dawn of the western world.

But if you were simply to be struck by how far back in the past it came to the West, you would still be missing the point—because the first tulkus not only happened to arrive at the time when western civilization was starting its unfolding.

They were the ones who had the power, and the compassion, to allow it to unfold.[25]

# 5

# The Endless Joy

AND NOW what we do is smooth the story, give it its finishing touches, then deposit it in open hiding among all the other things of nature—almost undetectable to anyone unaware, an object of unimaginable power for those in the future who will care to remember and remember to care.

Sometimes it can happen.

People peer out from behind their mental barricades and the fear is just too much. Even the best of academics simply panic at the prospect of any significant contacts between ancient Greeks and the dreadful emptinesses of Central Asia.

They groan, complain. And to try and disguise the centuries of unspeakable terror that should never be mentioned, they will come up with a hundred very sensible reasons why such interactions could never have taken place. It would all be much too difficult; the culture shock would be just too traumatic; the language obstacles would be quite insurmountable without a modern dictionary or decent training course; the distances would be impossible to cover without planes or trains or a rental car; the people would be hostile, the changes in climate way too extreme.

But there is one fine detail they always seem to miss: that if those who make history were like those who write it, nothing would ever happen. Those who make a difference do so because they are different, because they are prepared if necessary to walk thousands of miles; learn as many languages as needed word by word; ignore the warnings and rewrite the rules; push back the barriers of the impossible.[26]

And there is something else, too. There are also those humble facts that, if only given a chance, will speak far louder than the strongest fears.

While western historians try to insist that Greeks before the appearance of Alexander the Great would never have ventured more than the tiniest distance into inner Asia, archaeologists have been trying to explain something else—that not only hundreds but thousands of years earlier than Abaris, or Pythagoras, Europeans were already traveling out all the way across Central Asia into China.

And they would settle there, around the vast areas now known as the Tarim Basin that stretches down from below the Altai Mountains towards Tibet. Sometimes they settled alone, sometimes together with Mongolians.

Those were the days when East and West were in many ways even more closely linked than they are now:

the early days of what, a great deal later, would go by the name of the Silk Road.

The simple truth is that travel and trade routes reaching from China through to Europe were a physical reality long before the time of Pythagoras. And if you were to imagine Pythagoras himself sitting on some Greek island waiting patiently for Abaris, his toes dipped in the Mediterranean, you would be more than a little mistaken.

On the contrary, he had a reputation which spread far and wide for traveling to places so distant most Greeks had hardly even heard of them before. And when we look at the most tangible signs of all for where he traveled they point not to Egypt, or India.

They point not only eastwards but also northwards, towards the lands of the nomads and Central Asia.

With the people who were shaping our western world everything was moving, flowing. And far from fading away, the ripples of those interactions kept growing.

Roughly a hundred years after Pythagoras died and his original followers were scattered and the teaching center he had built up in southern Italy had been destroyed, there was just one remaining community of Italian Pythagoreans that still managed to blossom as well as survive. It was at a place known as Tarentum—with the famous Pythagorean inventor called Archytas as its spiritual, political, military leader.

And here at Tarentum a painted image was found. It had been created during the period of Archytas' rule; and it was the portrait of a Mongol.

In modern times perhaps just three or four people have even noticed this western portrait of a Mongol. Most of them were perfectly aware that there is nothing accidental about the fact it was discovered here, inside the only surviving stronghold of Pythagoreans, as opposed to anywhere else—considering Pythagoreanism's undying fascination with the Hyperborean ancestry of its master.

Even so, they were astonished at how small it shows us the ancient world really happened to be.

But after all we have seen about the origins and circlings of a certain ambassador, an Avar holding his arrow, the only thing left to be surprised at is why anyone would need to be surprised.[27]

The men and women who went by the name of Avars appeared, then disappeared, as mysteriously as Abaris himself.

For them, crossing Asia was like a walk in somebody's backyard. And with their web of influences and connections stretching over the centuries from Europe all the way to China, you might expect everyone would know a great deal about who they are.

But nobody knows anything of the kind. As for what they felt, saw, the songs they sang, they never had the slightest interest in leaving any signs or indications behind.

The name Avar was often the only thing that seemed to hold them together, to give them some constantly elusive sense of identity or continuity as they kept traveling and moving around. And as for their history: whatever you can read about them is not their history at all.

It simply is the story, written by outsiders, of how their enemies liked to perceive them.

For Avars themselves, history was the markings they left on the surface of the earth with their feet and hoofs. It was the intricately beautiful designs on their belts recording all the curvings of their ancestry. And as for what or who these barbarians were, that was just a mystery—sometimes self-contradicting, sometimes self-confirming—glimpsed by strangers here or there. Everything else is silence.

The leaders of their enemies out west were stunned, just like the Chinese, by the amazing slipperiness of their fighting techniques and the precision of their destructiveness. But they also were bewildered by their generosity and kindness, by their unexpected ability to be far more Christian than any Christian as they took care of ordinary people or looked after the poor or made sure to feed the armies sent out to destroy them.[28]

And it was the same story with the Mongols as a whole.

During the time of their first contacts with other cultures they lived by a code of honor and ethics no one else could even come close to. But not only were they singularly uninterested in presenting their side of the story: the most famous of their leaders was very careful to insist on being seen by his enemies in the worst conceivable light.

Through Genghis Khan destruction poured out from Mongolia. And something else poured out as well. Even among Muslims, harder hit than anyone by the waves of invasion, there were more than a few people acutely conscious of the paradoxical complexities they were facing—of a reality unfolding in front of their eyes compared to which all their civilized achievements faded into nothing, of a force grinding down the old fossilized forms of illusion to create the space for something new.

Sufis had visions of Genghis Khan's army being protected and led along its warpath by the most powerful of saints or even by the Pole, the supreme spiritual authority around whom the whole world revolves; or by the prophet Khidr, the Green Man, the mysterious guide of all guides who always acts from behind the scenes in ways that defy any human understanding.

And what they saw was profoundly true. The conquering Mongols appeared out of nowhere like a wildfire. But wildfires only burn to produce a greater growth and more gorgeous greenery than had ever been seen since the wildfire that came before. And as long as the Mongols kept faithful to their nomadic traditions they were able to perform the strangest alchemy.

Living apart from the great civilizations, treading their own different path, they managed to cross-fertilize civilizations and sow the seeds of new cultures in ways no individual culture could even dream of. Genghis Khan brought with him an all-embracing openness, a religious tolerance based on shamanic principles, that was almost as much of a threat to his enemies as anything else. He introduced not just the idea but the reality of international law and trade and travel, and helped lay the foundations for the modern world.[29]

But in his own way he was only repeating what already had taken place at the dawn of western culture: simply re-enacting the drama that plays itself out when we make our way back to the origins of what we know as the West and no longer find the West.

Instead a Mongol is standing there with an arrow, symbol of destruction, in his hand—ready, at precisely the right place and exactly the right time, to transmit the power needed for a new culture to come into being.

This is the impossible enigma that only a barbarous Mongol is fully able to embody. And this is the way things always will be, because civilizations are brought into existence out of a place of creation and destruction that no civilization by itself is ever able to understand.

There is no escaping the barbarians, because they are the life behind what we think of as life. And it was simply inevitable that this same mysterious pattern would be repeated, undetected, not only in the Old World but also in the New.

The sacred symbolism of the arrow was carried from Asia to North America: from the Mongols through to the Iroquois. Then, with the help of the Iroquois Confederacy as well as the Founding Fathers, its imagery went straight into creating the Great Seal of the United States while its essential message was taken into the United States Constitution.

And this happened to be far more than just a matter of imagery or symbols. What was being offered and transmitted was the life, the promise, at the heart of the new United States—provided of course that Americans would be ready to respect that life, protect its purity, honor its source.

But that brings us to a paradox as terrifying as any Mongol or barbarian. This is the paradox of how civilizations are so quick to identify with their own particular brand of life that, whether American or Tibetan or Persian or Greek, they never have the humility to identify the source of the life and oneness running through their veins.[30]

❖

He died in the same kind of felt tent he had been born in.

But no one would ever tell where Genghis Khan's body ended up after being taken back to Mongolia. They say he was buried under a tree with the most beautiful green leaves—he had selected it because of the pleasure and shelter it gave him out in the wilderness when he was younger—close to the sacred mountain he always considered his spiritual home.

Otherwise everything is silence: the body hidden away with strictest orders that the location of the burial would never be disclosed. There was nothing, not the slightest marker, to show the spot.

A vast area of land was sealed off in every direction all around. According to the practice and tradition of the Khans, it was called the Great Taboo. The whole region was constantly guarded by warriors. Anyone who happened to stumble inside it by accident was killed; so was anybody who deliberately tried getting into the area even just to create a little shrine, a place of worship. Nature was left to her own devices.

And this went on for almost eight hundred years.

Finally the Soviets arrived. But they had their own reasons for keeping everyone away, because they were terrified that the memory and heartland of Genghis Khan could become a focus for some national resistance. So the Great Taboo was given a new name—the Highly Restricted Area—and for good measure surrounded by another even more gigantic Restricted Area under the direct command and supervision of Moscow.

They carried out nuclear tests, dumped weapons, created a toxic junkyard. They added a big tank base so they could rest a little more assured that no one would ever slip inside by accident. Then they arrested, tortured, systematically killed every Mongol who even dared do any research into her or his own history.

And without a doubt you are bound to feel sure that nothing so exotic, so utterly foreign or monstrously barbaric, could ever exist in our modern western world. But the exact opposite is true, because we live under the shadow of a taboo so pervasive and well-guarded that even its name is kept secret. We have our own Great Taboo, our own Highly Restricted Area, except that almost nobody is ever allowed to become aware of its presence everywhere.

This is the taboo against discovering the sacred source of the world we live in: against finding what life is really for, against knowing why civilizations are born or die.

Even in the case of Genghis Khan, we understand almost nothing. He happened to be the most powerful man in the world; a constant innovator, superb commander; conqueror of more land and people and nations than anyone either before him or since. But he never made a major decision which had not already been made for him, and conveyed to him down to the smallest details, in a state of ecstasy.[31]

Of course this is not what people want to hear: they have their own ideas about what history is and should be. But we have already seen enough with Abaris, Hermotimus, Pythagoras, to be able to grasp that together they form part of a completely different story—a story waiting to be told again now, even if only briefly, because without it nothing has any real point.

And it goes like this.

Cultures are created and destroyed in ecstasy—and for every moment in between there is nothing that keeps a world alive aside from the breath of ecstatics.

People in general sincerely believe they know what life and the past and present are, although they know nothing. The news, the huge archives, the carefully written books are all about nothing. They are not even about the shadows of reality, or about moving chairs on the decks of a ship that soon could go down. They are absolutely nothing.

There is no such thing as true movement in this world. We can seem to run, push, dance, fly; make our way into space. But the only movement that really exists is the restlessness of our busy minds.

The whole of existence is an elaborate illusion to make everyone believe that something can be done here, even though nothing is ever done. In spite of all the personal dreams, the collective hopes and aspirations, nothing whatsoever is achieved because the real doing all happens somewhere else.

At any given point in time there will only ever be one single way to put a real step forward—which is in a state of ecstasy that takes us out of ourselves. This is how it always has been and will be for each of us; and this also is how it is for the whole.

We have the strange idea in the West that civilizations just happen: that they come into existence as a hit or miss affair and then we bumble along, creating and inventing and making it better.

But this is not how things are done at all.

Civilizations never just happen. They are brought into existence quite consciously, with unbelievable compassion and determination, from another world. Then the job of people experienced in ecstasy is to prepare the soil for them; carefully sow and plant them; care for them; watch them grow.

And each culture is just like a tree whose essence and whole potential are already contained in the seed. Nothing during the course of a civilization is ever discovered, or invented, or created, which was not already present inside that seed.

In our unconsciousness we take credit where no credit is due, oblivious to the real source of everything we pretend is ours—the sacred origin not just of religion but also of everything else, of science and technology, education and law, of medicine, logic, architecture, ordinary daily life, the cry of longing, the excruciating ache of the awakening love for wisdom.

And then there are those who quietly go about doing whatever is needed: the ones who wait in a state of ecstasy to help bring new civilizations into being, the ones without whom nothing is possible.

But not only are these people needed to bring new worlds into existence. They even are needed to bring them to an end so as to help make way for the new.

The simple truth is that every single civilization, including this western world, was brought into being from a sacred place to serve a sacred purpose. And when that purpose is forgotten, when its original alignment gets lost, when the fundamental balance and harmony of its existence become disrupted beyond a certain point, then nature has her way.

This is the mystery of birth and death not only for humans, but for cultures too. And for thousands of years it has been understood that, just as civilizations have to come to an end, there can even be times of global extinctions. But always there are people who know how to gather the essence of life and hold it safely, protect it and nurture it until the next seeding.[32]

They are the ones who are entrusted to turn the pages of life, to open the book of a culture and close it. They are the ones who are given permission to sound the note that will bring a new world into being and then sing the song that will bring it nearer to its close. They are the watchers who know the real meaning of responsibility and compassion—who are needed to witness the beginnings and endings because without the simple power of their attention nothing can ever be done.

And all we do is sometimes catch a glimpse of what they do without having the slightest clue about the process as a whole.

There are really only two kinds of people in existence. There is everyone who has been trained to live either for today or for tomorrow, stuck in all the cycles of endless preparations and expectations, dutifully digging holes and then falling into them, always busy trying to plant something fresh in the well-worn patterns of the old.

This is called waiting for the new moon.

And then there are those who know how to work in perfect stillness, imperceptibly bringing the future into being.

That is called waiting for the new sun.

There is an ancient myth from Central Asia that describes how civilizations are born.

It was known to the early Avars; to the distant ancestors of Tibetans as well as Mongols. This is the myth of the impenetrable mountains.

The people are completely stuck, cornered, hemmed in, the path ahead blocked by insurmountable obstacles rising in front of and all around them. There is no way forward, no hope.

And then the impossible happens. In one version a wild wolf finds them, feels compassion, shows them how to bore a hole through the solid rock into what will become their future. In another, the mysterious shaman shoots an arrow straight through the impenetrable mountains—creating what would come to be known as the arrow path.[33]

You could hardly think of a more straightforward myth. But it happens to contain the secret we in the West, with all our complications, have forgotten.

A new civilization, any civilization including ours, is not only a miraculous gift. It always comes into existence out of the impossible.

And the impossible is impossible: is absolutely non-negotiable. But however simple that may sound, nothing can be more essential for us to understand.

The world we now live in is a world of infinite possibilities—which is why it has no future. And there is no point in trying to kid ourselves that we know what the impossible is, because even the things we like to think of as impossible are simply the possibilities we decided to put aside.

The problem is that possibilities are nothing but finely modified, recalibrated versions of the old: the same recycling of the same. And they swallow whatever energy we have left, devour our intelligence, gobble our hopes and aspirations, cheat us of time until we no longer remember what life is about.

As we are we will never, not in a thousand years, not in our wildest dreams, find our way into the future. We are trapped on every side by possibilities.

And here is where this story comes in.

Nothing could seem more insubstantial or insignificant than such an inconceivably impossible story, waving and rippling like gossamer ahead of the wind, except for the fact that it will outlast you and me and the whole world we live in.

And although we may appear to have arrived at the end of this little incantation, there really is no end to it at all—any more than there is an end to the joy of being present with those who watch over and give birth to worlds.

And the point of life is to follow that presence wherever it leads; never to let it out of your sight; not to look aside even for a moment to the right or left; and once you hold it in your hand or inside your body, never to let it go until the time is right.

# Notes

**1.**

"And now…": this is the final couplet from Konstantinos Kavafis' *Perimenontas tous barbarous* or *Waiting for the barbarians* (where translators strangely neglect the fullness of meaning in Kavafis' last word, *lysis*), trans. Peter Kingsley. "The last stages …": *Wisdomkeepers*, ed. S. Wall and H. Arden (Hillsboro 1990) 95; this quotation © Steve Wall and Harvey Arden is reprinted with permission from Beyond Words Publishing, Hillsboro, Oregon.

**2.**

From the beginning Abaris is consistently called a Hyperborean (Herodotus, *Histories* 4.36; Plato, *Charmides* 158b, etc.). Only much later do we find writers (listed e.g. in G. Moravcsik, *Kőrösi Csoma-Archivum*, Supplementary volume 1/2, 1936, 105 n.4; J.F. Kindstrand, *Anacharsis*, Uppsala 1981, 18 n.5) occasionally describing him as a Scythian. J.N. Bremmer (*The rise and fall of the afterlife*, London 2002, 33) is mistaken both in stating that Abaris is referred to as a Scythian by Heraclides Ponticus, and also in ascribing this development specifically to association of Abaris with the Scythian Anarchasis. It simply is due to the fact that, for many Greek or Byzantine writers, the word "Scythian" covered foreigners from anywhere between the Black Sea and China. See e.g. S. West in *Brill's companion to Herodotus*, ed. E.J. Bakker et al. (Leiden 2002) 439; W. Pohl, *Die Awaren* (Munich 1988) 4–5 (add Theophylactus Simocatta, *History* 7.8.4 on Avars as "the most highly skilled among the Scythians" even though they were from Mongolia); and note Voltaire's passionate eighteenth-century attack on Genghis Khan as "a wild Scythian soldier" (*L'orphelin de la Chine*, Paris 1755; J. Weatherford, *Genghis Khan and the making of the modern world*, New York 2004, xxvi, 255). For examples of links between Scythian traditions as reported by ancient Greeks and the traditions of Mongolia cf. A. Alföldi, *Gnomon* 9 (1933) 566; S. West, *Museum Helveticum* 56 (1999) 78–82; and see e.g. A. Curry, *Science* 313 (08.25.2006) 1029 on Scythian presence in Mongolia. For Scythian culture and Tibet cf. J.V. Bellezza, *Zhang Zhung* (Vienna 2008) 93–100, 544–57.

On the opposite directions of Abaris' journey from Hyperborea and of the journey made by Aristeas from Proconnesus, near modern Istanbul at the eastern tip of Europe, into Central Asia see K.O. Müller's comments, *Geschichte der griechischen Literatur bis auf das Zeitalter Alexanders* i (Stuttgart 1882) 389–90; also J. Wiesner's, *Jahrbuch des Deutschen Archäologischen Instituts* 78 (1963) 214. For the Apollonian trance or ecstasy experienced by Aristeas as he traveled—"seized by Apollo," *phoibolamptos genomenos*—see Herodotus 4.13; J.D.P. Bolton, *Aristeas of Proconnesus* (Oxford 1962) 134–9; P. Kingsley, *In the dark places of wisdom* (Inverness, CA 1999) 112, 245. On the specific connotations of ecstasy contained in this word *phoibolamptos* see H. Hanse, *Gott haben* (Berlin 1939) 38; W. Burkert in *Apocalypticism in the Mediterranean world and the Near East*, ed. D. Hellholm (Tübingen 1983) 248–9; K. Dowden, *The uses of Greek mythology* (London 2005) 91. Stephanie West's unfortunate attempt at rationalizing the word in its application to Aristeas ("the sober determination of a pilgrim or missionary"; "a claim to special insight, beyond what is ordinarily granted to men": *Pontus and the outside world*, ed. C.J. Tuplin, Leiden 2004, 53 and 62) is impossible to justify—whether through an appeal to Plato's notorious habit of detaching religious terms from their original context by transposing them onto a "philosophical" level (for Plato on *numpholēptos* see W.R. Connor, *Classical antiquity* 7, 1988, 158–60 and, for the word's traditional meaning, P. Borgeaud in *Religions of the ancient world*, ed. S.I. Johnston, Cambridge, MA 2004, 412) or on any rational grounds whatsoever. When applied to Aristeas, the expression *phoibolamptos genomenos* serves as a precise functional parallel to the expression *enthous genomenos* which is specifically applied to the ecstatic journeying of Abaris (Lycurgus fr. 85 Blass = XIV.5 Conomis): on the interconnections between *enthous* and *phoibolamptos* see e.g. Hanse 35–8 with 38 n.2; Bolton 136. For a long time it has been routine to group Abaris and Aristeas together: cf. e.g. Iamblichus, *Pythagorean life* 138; C.A. Lobeck, *Aglaophamus* (Königsberg 1829) i 313–14; M. Eliade, *Shamanism* (Princeton 1962) 388–9; W. Burkert, *Lore and science in ancient Pythagoreanism* (Cambridge, MA 1972) 147–50, 162; and see also M.L. West, *The Orphic poems* (Oxford 1983) 54 n.63 (Abaris and the Issedonians). As a reminder of the deep cultural unity linking ancient Siberia, Mongolia, Tibet and China see C. Ginzburg's comments, *Ecstasies* (New York 1991) 289 n.209; also J.V. Bellezza, *Spirit-mediums, sacred mountains and related Bon textual traditions in Upper Tibet* (Leiden 2005), esp. 20–21, and *Zhang Zhung* 543–59. For Aristeas, the Altai and Central Asia on the way to Hyperborea cf. B. Laufer, *T'oung Pao* 9 (1908) 449, 452; E.H. Minns, *Scythians and Greeks* (Cambridge 1913) 110–14; Moravcsik 110–12; E.R. Dodds, *The Greeks and the irrational* (Berkeley 1951) 141, 162; J. Needham, *Science and civilisation in China* i (Cambridge 1954) 170–2, 186, 248; E.D. Phillips, *Artibus Asiae* 18 (1955) 161–77 and 20 (1957) 159–62; Bolton 74–118; Wiesner 202, 209–13; Burkert, *Lore* 162; P. Lindegger, *Griechische und römische Quellen zum Peripheren Tibet* i (Rikon 1979) 86–94; J. Ferguson in *Aufstieg und Niedergang der römischen Welt* II 9,2 (Berlin 1980) 581-2; M.G. Raschke, ibid. 610, 692; C.A.P. Ruck in R.G. Wasson et al., *Persephone's quest* (New Haven 1986) 226–8; M.A. Levi, *I nomadi alla frontiera* (Rome 1989) 83, 90–2; H.-G. Nesselrath, *Museum Helveticum* 52 (1995) 27 n.11; Kingsley, *Dark places* 113–14, 245; J.P. Mallory and V.H. Mair, *The Tarim mummies* (London 2000) 39–45, 53–4 with P.S. MacDonald, *History of the concept of mind* i (Farnham 2003) 24 n.45; Z.S. Samašev et al., *Eurasia antiqua* 8 (2002) 272–3; also G. Azarpay, *Artibus Asiae* 22 (1959) 313–14 and A. Alemany i Vilamajó, *Faventia* 21 / 2 (1999) 45–55. On the location of Hyperborea to the east, as well as north, of Greece see Needham i 170–2; Bolton 115–116; Ruck 227. Bremmer's absurd attempts to refute the existence of any real ties between Aristeas' journey and Central Asia are as parochial in their motivation as they are futile, while his simplistic dismissal of the famous account about gold-guarding griffins as nothing but "a doublet replacing ants with griffins" (*The early Greek concept of the soul*, Princeton 1983, 36–7; *Rise and fall* 33) is remarkable in its arbitrariness and disrespect for the evidence. On Bremmer's marked penchant for "sleight of hand" (an expression that, ironically, he applies to others: *Rise and fall* 34) see M.L. West's broad comments, *Classical Review* 35

(1985) 56–8 with P. Kingsley, *Studia Iranica* 23 (1994) 190–1, and for Aristeas' griffins cf. e.g. Lindegger 54 n.4, 84 n.6, 87–8; A. Mayor and M. Heaney, *Folklore* 104 (1993) 40–66 with A. Mayor, *The first fossil hunters* (Princeton 2000) 22–7; Nesselrath 23–7; N.V. Polosmak, *Siberian archaeological herald* 1 (1997); J. Davis-Kimball and M. Behan, *Warrior women* (New York 2002) 79, 96–111; also H.W. Haussig, *Byzantion* 23 (1953) 358–9. Andreas Alföldi (566–7; cf. Bolton 82–3) already saw the links between Aristeas' one-eyed Arimaspians and Mongolian traditions long before modern translations had become readily available of the *Secret history of the Mongols*, which gives one-eyed people a key role in the origins of the Mongol race (*The secret history of the Mongols* §4, trans. P. Kahn and F.W. Cleaves, 2nd ed., Boston 1998, 3; D. Ermakov, *Bo and Bön*, Kathmandu 2008, 679 n.279). Bremmer also insisted on denying any legitimate background in Asiatic shamanism for the accounts of Aristeas, or his soul, being transformed into a raven (Herodotus 4.15; Pliny, *Natural history* 7.174; *Early Greek concept* 35). But see now Marjorie Mandelstam Balzer in *American anthropologist* 98 (1996) 305–18—whose tears say all that is needed.

## 3.

For Abaris = "the Avar" see e.g. the entry in the *Suda* s.v. *Abaris* (A18 Adler); A. Bonfini, *Rerum Ungaricarum decades* (Basel 1568) 11; R.G. Latham in *A dictionary of Greek and Roman geography*, ed. W. Smith, i (London 1878) 350; G. Moravcsik, *Kőrösi Csoma-Archivum*, Supplementary volume 1/2 (1936) 104–18; H.Z. Koşay, *Türk Tarih Kurumu tarafından yapılan Alaca Höyük kazısı 1937–1939* (Ankara 1951) 91, 185; G. László, *The art of the migration period* (Coral Gables 1974) 41; H.W. Bailey, *Bulletin of the School of Oriental and African Studies* 42 (1979) 210; W. Pohl, *Die Awaren* (Munich 1988) 31, 38; L. Rásonyi, *Doğu Avrupada Türklük* (Istanbul 2006) 42. Of course even in modern Greek the letter "b" is still pronounced as a "v." As for someone being given the personal name "Avar" by Greeks: it should hardly need saying that difficulties in communication due to differences of language can make this kind of confusion almost inevitable when first introducing or identifying oneself to foreigners. But we also need to consider the more specific fact that Avars were not nearly as fond as Greeks were (or we now are) of giving out their personal names in public. They often preferred identifying themselves very broadly in terms of their tribe or their useful function in life, making outsiders mistake for a personal name what was just an Avar's impersonal description or title: cf. W. Pohl in *Nomen et gens*, ed. D. Geuenich et al. (Berlin 1997) 84–90. This same tendency is also reflected in Avars' avoidance of giving individual names to their places of power, which are referred to instead by the simple title "place of the Avars" (Pohl in *Topographies of power in the early Middle Ages*, ed. M. de Jong et al., Leiden 2001, 458–9). With regard to the more general phenomenon of a tribe's name also being given as a personal name to individuals, see e.g. P.B. Golden in *Aspects of Altaic civilization III: Proceedings of the thirtieth meeting of the Permanent International Altaistic Conference*, ed. D. Sinor (Bloomington 1990) 37–8 with n.22; O. Karatay in *Ērān ud Anērān*, ed. M. Compareti (Venice 2006) 361; and note also Paul the Deacon, *History of the Lombards* 1.27. For another example of a name appearing both in Herodotus and among the Avars see Pohl, *Awaren* 38, 187 and in *Nomen et gens* 89 (Targitius). And for the, to us often amazing, consistency of Asiatic traditions over periods of many centuries cf. e.g. S. West, *Journal of Hellenic studies* 108 (1988) 208; F. Thordarson, *Symbolae Osloenses* 72 (1997) 91–3; P. Kingsley, *In the dark places of wisdom* (Inverness, CA 1999) 165–7; J. Davis-Kimball, *Ancient West and East* 1 (2002) 345; below, note 8.

On the origin of the Avars in Mongolia see A. Alföldi, *Eurasia septentrionalis antiqua* 9 (1934) 289–92; P. Lipták, *Acta archaeologica Academiae Scientiarum Hungaricae* 10 (1959) 251–79 and *Avars and ancient Hungarians* (Budapest 1983); R. Grousset, *The empire of the steppes* (New Brunswick 1970) xxiii, 66–7, 171–6, 193; K.H. Menges in *Encyclopaedia Iranica* v (New York 1973) 910a; László 41; K. Czeglédy, *Archivum Eurasiae medii aevi* 3 (1983) 25–125; C.I. Beckwith, *The Tibetan empire in Central Asia* (Princeton 1987) 178 and *Empires of the Silk Road* (Princeton 2009) 103–4, 113–15, 390–1, 406–7; P.B. Golden, *An introduction to the history of the Turkic peoples* (Wiesbaden 1992) 72, 76–9, 108–111; E.G. Pulleyblank, *Migracijske teme* 15 (1999) 37, 44, 55 and *Journal of Chinese Linguistics* 27 (1999)

153; E. Helimski, *Folia orientalia* 36 (2000) 135–48; E. Heršak in *The Turks*, ed. H.C. Güzel et al., i (Ankara 2002) 590–1; M. Stachowski, *Studia etymologica Cracoviensia* 9 (2004) 133–41; and for their origins in what Chinese authors called "the northern wilderness" cf. e.g. Du You, *Tongdian* 196 (Zhonghua Shuju edition, Beijing 1988, 5378: Rouran). When mentioning Mongols in this book I will be referring very broadly to the nomads of the Mongol plateau who also were tribal and cultural ancestors of what later would become the Mongol nation—not passing any judgement on the infinitely intricate question of whether, from a much more technical point of view, they happen to be what specialists nowadays like to describe as "proto-Mongolic" or "archaic-Turkic." On the virtual silence of early Chinese sources about the nomadic peoples living at or just beyond China's northern borders see Pulleyblank's comments, *Migracijske teme* 15 (1999) 36, 41; and cf. also Czeglédy 120 with N. Di Cosmo's observations, *Ancient China and its enemies* (Cambridge 2002) 281–4.

## 4.

Skywalker: cf. S. Chandra Das, *A Tibetan English dictionary* (Calcutta 1902) 180b (*khandro*) with J.É. Kowalewski, *Dictionnaire mongol-russe-français* i (Kasan 1844) 432b; J. van Durme, *Mélanges chinois et bouddhiques* 1 (1931–32) 274 n.2; M. Eliade, *Shamanism* (Princeton 1962) 410; H.V. Guenther, *The royal song of Saraha* (Berkeley 1973) 79 n.9. Skywalker as arrow: Chandra Das 180b. It will be noted that although Sanskrit *ḍāka* and *ḍākinī* are often translated nowadays as "skywalker," this is not what the words themselves originally mean (for the history of the explanation cf. D.B. Gray, *The Cakrasamvara tantra*, New York 2007, 85); the artificial etymologizing of *ḍākinī* as meaning *ākāśagāminī* (A. Herrmann-Pfandt, *Ḍākinīs*, Bonn 1992, 115) never made an impact in India outside of scholarly circles and, like *khecarī*, is clearly a reflex of older shamanic traditions. For Abaris as "skywalker" (*aithrobatēs*) see Porphyry, *Life of Pythagoras* 29; Iamblichus, *Pythagorean life* 136; C. Saerens in *Studia varia Bruxellensia ad orbem graeco-latinum pertinentia* iii, ed. Saerens et al. (Leuven 1994) 154; P. Kingsley, *In the dark places of wisdom*

(Inverness, CA 1999) 112, 245 (on the meaning of *aithēr* cf. Kingsley, *Ancient philosophy, mystery and magic*, Oxford 1995, 15–23: Tibetan *khandro* can, equally well, be translated as "ether–walker"). The Greek word "smokewalker," *kapnobatēs*, has a similar construction but a different meaning (Strabo, *Geography* 7.3.3, applied to ritual Thracian cannabis smokers; cf. also R.D. Edmunds, *The Shawnee prophet*, Lincoln, NE 1985, 53–4). As for Aristophanes' use of the word "cloudwalking" to describe the effects of Socrates' teaching, it obviously is a mocking distortion of these exotic names (see *Clouds* 225 and 1503 *aerobatō*; A. Willi, *The language of Aristophanes*, Oxford 2003, 114). For another example of this type of word formation in east Asia, compare the "cloud–ladders" of the Mongols and Chinese (T.T. Allsen, *Archivum Eurasiae medii aevi* 7, 1987–91, 20 n.49; Jieming Liang, *Chinese siege warfare*, Singapore 2006, 111). On George Lucas' massive reading of books about eastern mythology and religion in preparation for his *Star Wars*, see e.g. K.S. Decker et al., *Star Wars and philosophy* (Chicago 2005) 145 n.2. Joseph Campbell's influence on Lucas is well known, as are the many Tibetan linguistic and mythological features that became incorporated into the *Star Wars* films.

## 5.

Abaris' arrow as a dart: Lycurgus fr. 85 Blass = XIV.5 Conomis (*belos*). Bulky: Heraclides Ponticus fr. 51c Wehrli (*hupermegethēs*). Made of gold: Iamblichus, *Pythagorean life* 141 (*oïston chrusoun*). On the ancestry of the Iamblichus passage see W. Burkert, *Lore and science in ancient Pythagoreanism* (Cambridge, MA 1972) 143 n.127 with note 10 below.

A remark by the Greek orator Lycurgus is repeatedly mistranslated in modern scholarly literature as stating that Abaris carried an arrow because arrows used to be a standard "symbol" or attribute of Apollo. But Lycurgus is making the much more specific point that Abaris was given his arrow as a special "token" from Apollo (fr. 85 Blass, *sumbolon echōn to belos tou Apollōnos*: for *sumbolon* here cf. e.g. Lysias, *Speeches* 19.25; for *symbolon* in general see P. Kingsley, *Ancient philosophy, mystery and magic*, Oxford

95

1995, 289–90; and for arrows as tokens, the references in notes 6 and 7 below). The fact is that, although Apollo was a great archer god for the Greeks and was famous for his deadly arrows, his attribute and symbol were not the arrow but the bow: M.P. Nilsson, *Geschichte der griechischen Religion* i (3rd ed., Munich 1967) 541; H. Kothe, *Klio* 52 (1970) 206 n.7. When Apollo is very occasionally shown in the Middle East with an arrow instead of a bow, this is the clear result of Iranian and Asiatic influence: H. Gesche, *Jahrbuch für Numismatik und Geldgeschichte* 19 (1969) 50 with n.25, 52 with n.39. In trying to find a parallel for Abaris with his solitary arrow, Bremmer logically ended up turning to Siberia (*The early Greek concept of the soul*, Princeton 1983, 45; for his mention of the Finnish *Kalevala* see W. Heissig's comments in *Religion, myth and folklore in the world's epics*, ed. L. Honko, Berlin 1990, 455–70 about the epic's very conspicuous Mongolian and shamanic affinities). As if to underscore the uniqueness and strangeness of Abaris' arrow from a western point of view, sources in late antiquity finally manage to supply him with a bow and even a quiver to accompany it (Himerius, *Speeches* 23). But this is no more than one minor detail in the increasingly artificial portrayal of him as an ideal, stereotypical Scythian gentleman and warrior (A. Dyroff, *Philologus* 59, 1900, 613–14). We find the same kind of gravitation towards loose stereotypes and associative thinking in Ovid's mention of a fictitious *Caucasius Abaris*, where "Caucasian" has come to mean little more than "Scythian" (*Metamorphoses* 5.86; cf. F.D. Allen, *American journal of philology* 13, 1892, 55 n.3 with note 2 above; also G.H. Macurdey, *Classical review* 34, 1920, 139); and the fact is that, although people in Ovid's time may have had a fair enough idea of where the Caucasus started, as a rule they had no clear notion as to exactly where inside of Asia it might have ended (R. Hennig, *Terrae incognitae* i, 2nd ed., Leiden 1944, 183 n.2, 195; J.D.P. Bolton, *Aristeas of Proconnesus*, Oxford 1962, 50–3, 176–82; G. Parker, *The making of Roman India*, Cambridge 2008, 87, 230).

**6.**

On the crafting of arrows by Mongols, and their use in hunting and war, see K.U. Köhalmi, *Acta orientalia Academiae Scientiarum Hungaricae* 3 (1953) 45–72 and 6 (1956) 109–162. For the primacy of the arrow in relation to the bow see ibid. 110–13 along with B. Adler in *Der Weltkreis* 2 (1931) 102, and on the whistling or piping sound of arrows cf. also B.E. Wallacker, *Oriens* 11 (1958) 181–2; I. de Rachewiltz, *The secret history of the Mongols* (Leiden 2004) i 437–8; J. Weatherford, *Genghis Khan and the making of the modern world* (New York 2004) 22, 72. For the deep symbolism attached to arrowmaking in Tibet see e.g. H.V. Guenther, *The royal song of Saraha* (Berkeley 1973) 5–7; K.R. Schaeffer, *Dreaming the great Brahmin* (New York 2005) 19–27; below, note 11. On the Avars' use of sound in battle see the *Suda* s.v. *lukēthmos*; M. Whitby, *The Emperor Maurice and his historian* (Oxford 1988) 84. For the practice of war as harmony in Pythagorean tradition cf. P. Kingsley, *Ancient philosophy, mystery and magic* (Oxford 1995) 146–7; and for the cosmic as well as ecstatic significance of the sound of piping or whistling, plus its connection with Apollo, *In the dark places of wisdom* (Inverness, CA 1999) 116–35.

Arrow as symbol or token of power among the Avars: G. László, *Études archéologiques sur l'histoire de la société des Avars* (Budapest 1955) 291; I. Bóna, *Acta archaeologica Academiae Scientiarum Hungaricae* 23 (1971) 312; S. Szádeczky-Kardoss in *The Cambridge history of early Inner Asia*, ed. D. Sinor (Cambridge 1990) 226; W. Pohl in *Nomen et gens*, ed. D. Geuenich et al. (Berlin 1997) 88; H. Steuer in *Reallexikon der germanischen Altertumskunde* xvii (2nd ed., Berlin 2004) 81a. See, in general, E.H. Parker, *A thousand years of the Tartars* (Shanghai 1895) 184; J. Harmatta, *Acta archaeologica Academiae Scientiarum Hungaricae* 1 (1951) 116–18; H. Serruys, *Journal of the American Oriental Society* 78 (1958) 279–94; H. Gesche, *Jahrbuch für Numismatik und Geldgeschichte* 19 (1969) 52; H. Göckenjan, *Acta orientalia Academiae Scientiarum Hungaricae* 58 (2005) 59–76.

7.

Abaris as ambassador: Harpocration = the *Suda* s.v. *Abaris* (*presbeuomenōn de pollōn ethnōn … kai Abarin ex Huperboreōn presbeutēn aphikesthai*); cf. also the scholia to Aristophanes' *Knights* 729a Mervyn Jones–Wilson (*elthonta theōron eis tēn Hellada*), and note 19 below.

Golden arrows in the early Khaganate: *Zhou Shu* 50 (Zhonghua Shuju edition, Beijing 1971, 910); Lin Ying, *Transoxiana* 6 (July 2003). In Tibet: *Jiu Tang Shu* 196.1 (Zhonghua Shuju edition, Beijing 1975, 5219). And for a much later example from the Manchu dynasty in China, which is a clear indicator of Mongol tradition (see e.g. H. Serruys, *Journal of the American Oriental Society* 78, 1958, 281), cf. C.G. Seligman, *Eurasia Septentrionalis antiqua* 9 (1934) 351; J. Harmatta, *Acta archaeologica Academiae Scientiarum Hungaricae* 1 (1951) 118. For golden arrows see also R. de Nebesky-Wojkowitz, *Oracles and demons of Tibet* (The Hague 1956) 16, 294; K. Meuli, *Gesammelte Schriften* (Basel 1975) ii 861–2 (Voguls, Siberia); O.J. Maenchen-Helfen, *Oriens* 10 (1957) 282 (Tashtyk and Pazyryk, Siberia); A. Vinogradov, *Ak Jang in the context of Altai religious tradition* (master's thesis, University of Saskatchewan 2003) Appendix 2 §9; R. Aggarwal, *Beyond lines of control* (Durham, NC 2004) 191 with J.G. Georgi, *Russia* iv (London 1783) 70 (the sacred golden arrow of Gesar Khan: on the origins of the Gesar epic cf. G.N. Roerich, *Izbrannye trudy*, Moscow 1967, 181–9). Golden bows: G. László, *Acta archaeologica Academiae Scientiarum Hungaricae* 1 (1951) 91–100; Harmatta 107–51; W. Heissig, *Erzählstoffe rezenter mongolischer Heldendichtung* (Wiesbaden 1988) 99; H. Göckenjan, *Acta orientalia Academiae Scientiarum Hungaricae* 58 (2005) 66, 68–9. Golden bows and silver arrows: O. Turan, *Belleten* IX / 35 (1945) 305–18. For golden quivers among the Avars see G. László, *Études archéologiques sur l'histoire de la société des Avars* (Budapest 1955) 291; Göckenjan 72; also S. Szádeczky-Kardoss in *The Cambridge history of early Inner Asia*, ed. D. Sinor (Cambridge 1990) 226; and cf. C. Brockelmann, *Ural-Altaische Jahrbücher* 24 (1952) 140–1 (Tashtyk, Siberia). As the Avars gave up their nomadic ways, and their dependence on archery, the great symbol of power and rank became a golden sword (R. Ghirshman, *Artibus Asiae* 26, 1963, 309; H. Nickel, *Metropolitan*

*Museum Journal* 7, 1973, 135 n.9). On the sacred symbolism of gold for Mongols see T.T. Allsen, *Commodity and exchange in the Mongol empire* (Cambridge 1997) 60–3: these sacred connotations need always to be borne in mind when considering the notorious importance of gold for Avars (W. Pohl, *Die Awaren*, Munich 1988, 178–82; A. Barbero, *Charlemagne*, Berkeley 2004, 70–1; M. Hardt, *Gold und Herrschaft*, Berlin 2004; and cf. the tradition about Abaris in Iamblichus, *Pythagorean life* 91–2, 141).

For some general comments on the long-standing Mongol tradition of envoys carrying arrows "as proof of the authenticity of the mission" see Serruys 279–82, 292. It also will be noted that, according to the symbolism of the Khaganate, an arrow is carried by an ambassador or envoy because he is himself an arrow shot on its mission by the great Khan who is the bow (cf. Harmatta 130–2; J.-P. Roux, *Turcica* 9, 1977, 24–7; also Göckenjan 71; and for the underlying principle see *The secret history of the Mongols* §124, trans. P. Kahn and F.W. Cleaves, 2nd ed., Boston 1998, 46.3–4). On the connection between the Avars and the origin of the Khans see e.g. P.B. Golden, *An introduction to the history of the Turkic peoples* (Wiesbaden 1992) 72.

**8.**
Abaris as healer and purifier: Iamblichus, *Pythagorean life* 91–2 (*katharmous ... katharmon*) with the *Suda* s.v. *Abaris* (*Katharmous*); C.A. Lobeck, *Aglaophamus* (Königsberg 1829) i 313; J.F. Kindstrand, *Anacharsis* (Uppsala 1981) 22–3; A.M. Bowie, *Aristophanes: myth, ritual and comedy* (Cambridge 1993) 121. For Abaris, together with his arrow, as a prophet see e.g. Lycurgus fr. 85 Blass = XIV.5 Conomis and the passages cited below from Apollonius, *Amazing stories* 4 (= *Paradoxographorum Graecorum reliquiae*, ed. A. Giannini, Milan 1965, 122), Iamblichus, *Pythagorean life* 135 and 141. Abaris as protector from plagues: Lycurgus, loc. cit. (*loimou*); Apollonius, *Amazing stories* 4 (*loimous ... loimos*); Harpocration = *Suda* s.v. *Abaris* (*loimou*); Iamblichus, *Pythagorean life* 91–2 (*loimous ... loimōxai*), 135–6 (*loimōn*) = Porphyry, *Life of Pythagoras* 29 (see note 19 below), 141 (*loimon ... loimon*). Of course for Greeks this is one more feature

99

connecting him with Apollo (M.P. Nilsson, *Geschichte der griechischen Religion* i, 3$^{rd}$ ed., Munich 1967, 541–3; C.A. Faraone, *Talismans and Trojan horses*, New York 1992). For Abaris as shaman cf. e.g. K. Meuli, *Gesammelte Schriften* (Basel 1975) ii 859–65; E.D. Phillips, *Artibus Asiae* 18 (1955) 177 n.85; J.-P. Roux, *Turcica* 9 (1977) 9 with n.9; H.W. Bailey, *Bulletin of the School of Oriental and African Studies* 42 (1979) 210. It will be noted that, to Avars, the single concept and perhaps even the single word "shaman–ambassador" will have been something quite familiar: G. Németh in *Turcologica. K semidesjatiletiju akademika A. N. Kononova*, ed. S. G. Kljaštornyj et al. (Leningrad 1976) 300 (*Qam-Sauči*).

Freedom from plagues: Theophylactus Simocatta, *History* 7.8.13 (… *phasi gar anōthen autous kai ex archēs mēdepote loimōn epidēmian theasasthai* …); H.W. Haussig, *Byzantion* 23 (1953) 284.22–7, 381–8; *The History of Theophylact Simocatta*, trans. M. and M. Whitby (Oxford 1986) 191. Modern commentators on this passage miss the point (especially clear in the words *anōthen … kai ex archēs*) that we are dealing not so much with statistical statements about the rarity of epidemics as with shamans' confident claims to be able to provide, through prophecy, unlimited immunity from plagues. See, immediately below, Theophylactus 7.8.15 on shaman–priests' abilities to predict the future (*hiereis kektēmenoi hoi kai tēn tōn mellontōn autois dokousin ektithesthai proagoreusin*: cf. Haussig 359 n.310; W. Pohl, *Die Awaren*, Munich 1988, 200) together with the routine Greek accounts of Abaris' divinatory ability to avoid plagues by predicting them (*proelegen de kai houtos seismous kai loimous kai ta paraplēsia*: Apollonius, *Amazing stories* 4; *prorrēseis te seismōn aparabatoi kai loimōn apotropai sun tachei … kai Abarin … toiauta tina epitetelekenai*: Iamblichus, *Pythagorean life* 135; *prolegōn loimon*: ibid. 141; cf. Nilsson 541–4). It will be noted that Mongols traditionally maintained harmony, health and balance in their surroundings through geomantic siting techniques based on the divinatory use of arrows: see Hok-Lam Chan, *Asia Major* 4/2 (1991) 53–78 and *Legends of the building of old Peking* (Hong Kong 2008), esp. 242–7. For the divinatory use of arrows by Mongol shamans cf. also V.M. Mikhailovskii, *Journal of the Anthropological Institute of Great Britain and Ireland* 24 (1895) 69, 96, 99. In Tibet:

R. de Nebesky-Wojkowitz, *Oracles and demons of Tibet* (The Hague 1956) 16–17, 365–7, 543–4; T. Ellingson, *Anthropology and humanism* 23 (1998) 51–76. And for the traditional role of Mongol shamans as protectors against epidemics, which "are let loose by powers malevolent to man," see W. Heissig's comments, *The religions of Mongolia* (London 1980) 9.

Shamanism of the Avars: *Suda* s.v. *dioptēres*; E.H. Parker, *Asiatic quarterly review* 13 (1902) 346, 353, 360, and 17 (1904) 140; Haussig 359–60; A. Kollautz, *Palaeologia* IV.3/4 (Osaka 1955) 285–95; R. Grousset, *The empire of the steppes* (New Brunswick 1970) 172; I. Bóna, *Acta archaeologica Academiae Scientiarum Hungaricae* 23 (1971) 283–4, 316–19; Pohl 38–9, 194, 199–203; S. Szádeczky-Kardoss in *The Cambridge history of early Inner Asia*, ed. D. Sinor (Cambridge 1990) 228; E. Heršak in *The Turks*, ed. H.C. Güzel et al., i (Ankara 2002) 594; B. Genito and L. Mádaras, *Archaeological remains of a steppe people in the Hungarian great plain* (Naples 2005) 78–82; L. Rásonyi, *Doğu Avrupada Türklük* (Istanbul 2006) 351–6. The magical creation of heavy rain before or during battles as a military technique for disorienting and overpowering the enemy, which the *Suda* (loc. cit.) explicitly attributes to Avars, is a very traditional practice of Mongol shamans (see *The secret history of the Mongols* §143, trans. P. Kahn and F.W. Cleaves, 2nd ed., Boston 1998, 55.21–33; C. Humphrey in *Shamanism, history and the state*, ed. N. Thomas and Humphrey, Ann Arbor 1994, 206; D. Christian, *A history of Russia, Central Asia and Mongolia* i, Oxford 1998, 256; I. de Rachewiltz, *The secret history of the Mongols*, Leiden 2004, i 525; D. Ermakov, *Bo and Bön*, Kathmandu 2008, 90). This reference in the *Suda*, a Byzantine Greek encyclopedia, to the Avars using such a technique provides the missing link—overlooked by J.J. Emerson in his otherwise interesting study *The secret history of the Mongols and western literature* (Sino-Platonic papers 135, Philadelphia 2004)—that joins Mongolian traditions to the mythological world of Merlin and Arthur. For another use by Avars of shamanism in warfare cf. Heršak 594. The remarkable conservatism over many centuries of Mongolian shamanic traditions, in particular, has often been commented on: see for example J.A. Boyle, *Folklore* 83 (1972) 177–93; S. Jagchid and P. Hyer, *Mongolia's culture and society* (Boulder 1979) 164–5;

R. Davidson, *Numen* 54 (2007) 358; V.H. Mair, *Eurasian studies* 6 (2007) 37. For the antiquity of shamanism as a religious and cultural phenomenon cf. e.g. J. van Durme, *Mélanges chinois et bouddhiques* 1 (1931–32) 268-9; W. Ruben, *Acta orientalia* 18 (1940) 205; F. Altheim, *Niedergang der alten Welt* (Frankfurt 1952) i 70; J. Maringer, *History of religions* 17 (1977) 105; Heissig 6–7, 17; J.E. Mitchiner, *Traditions of the seven Ṛṣis* (Delhi 1982) 188-9; P. Gignoux in *Orientalia Iosephi Tucci memoriae dicata*, ed. G. Gnoli and L. Lanciotti (Rome 1987) 507, and *Man and cosmos in ancient Iran* (Rome 2001) 73–8, 85–94; C. Ginzburg, *Ecstasies* (New York 1991) 208 (J.N. Bremmer, *The rise and fall of the afterlife*, London 2002, 30–1 with n.22, strangely omits any mention of the drum in this find at Pazyryk, no doubt because according to the criteria he himself has just established it would altogether undermine his own skeptical stance); P. Kingsley, *Studia Iranica* 23 (1994) 187–98 and *Ancient philosophy, mystery and magic* (Oxford 1995) 40–1, 222–7; H.-P. Francfort in *The archaeology of rock-art*, ed. C. Chippindale and P.S.C. Taçon (Cambridge 1998) 313; Y. Ustinova, *The supreme gods of the Bosporan kingdom* (Leiden 1999) 76–9; J. Davis-Kimball, *Ancient West and East* 1 (2002) 344–5; O. Purev and G. Purvee, *Mongolian shamanism* (Ulaanbaatar 2004) 13, 17–23; J.V. Bellezza, *Spirit-mediums, sacred mountains and related Bon textual traditions in Upper Tibet* (Leiden 2005), 20–1 and *Zhang Zhung* (Vienna 2008) 551–68; W. Burkert, *Kleine Schriften* iii (Göttingen 2006) 190; Mair 28; L. Grosman et al., *Proceedings of the National Academy of Sciences of the United States of America* 105/46 (November 18, 2008) 17665–9; below, note 25. The bright young theorist K. von Stuckrad has tried to posit the impossibility of any meaningful continuity between ancient religious phenomena and contemporary shamanic traditions (*Schamanismus und Esoterik*, Leuven 2003, 106–16). This all seems very logical; but according to the same logic von Stuckrad should of course never claim to have written or published anything, because he is a different person every year and every day.

## 9.

On the magical use of arrows in Mongolian, Tibetan and Siberian shamanism see V.M. Mikhailovskii, *Journal of the Anthropological Institute of Great Britain and Ireland* 24 (1895) 66, 69, 84, 96, 99, 128, 134–5; B. Adler, *Der Weltkreis* 2 (1931) 101–113; G. Moravcsik, *Kőrösi Csoma-Archivum*, Supplementary volume 1/2 (1936) 117; J. Harmatta, *Acta archaeologica Academiae Scientiarum Hungaricae* 1 (1951) 130; A. Kollautz, *Palaeologia* IV.3/4 (Osaka 1955) 291; K.U. Köhalmi, *Acta orientalia Academiae Scientiarum Hungaricae* 6 (1956) 123, 150; R. de Nebesky-Wojkowitz, *Oracles and demons of Tibet* (The Hague 1956) 16–17, 355, 365–8, 515, 543–4; C.R. Bawden, *Bulletin of the School of Oriental and African Studies* 25 (1962) 91–2 n.4, 92 with n.3, 100, 102; M. Eliade, *Shamanism* (Princeton 1962) 43 and in *Religions in antiquity: essays in memory of Erwin Ramsdell Goodenough*, ed. J. Neusner (Leiden 1968) 463–75; K. Meuli, *Gesammelte Schriften* (Basel 1975) ii 859 n.4; G. Ashe, *The ancient wisdom* (London 1977) 170 with V. LePage, *Shambhala* (Wheaton, IL 1996) 79; J.-P. Roux, *Turcica* 9 (1977) 9, 12; J.F. Kindstrand, *Anacharsis* (Uppsala 1981) 22; Hok-Lam Chan, *Asia Major* 4/2 (1991) 76 n.43; C. Humphrey and U. Onon, *Shamans and elders* (Oxford 1996) 23, 208, 348; L.P. Potapov, *Anthropology of consciousness* 10/4 (1999) 26, 30; H. Göckenjan, *Acta orientalia Academiae Scientiarum Hungaricae* 58 (2005) 59–76.

Arrows that clear their own path and steer themselves: Adler 102; Göckenjan 61; also R. Aggarwal, *Beyond lines of control* (Durham, NC 2004) 191 with 262 n.11; and for arrows as conscious and intelligent beings cf. Roux 8–9, 12. Note, too, the traditional role of the drum in Siberian shamanism which not only carried shamans on their journeys through the universe but also magically overcame all obstacles such as "when in the course of the journey the shaman's path was blocked by a river"—in just the same way that Abaris' arrow is described as overcoming all obstacles, especially rivers, that blocked his path. See Potapov 25 for the Siberian material; Iamblichus, *Pythagorean life* 91 (*epochoumenos gar autōi kai ta abata diebainen hoion potamous ...*) and 136 = Porphyry, *Life of Pythagoras* 29 (*aithrobatēs ... oïstōi ... epochoumenos potamous te kai pelagē kai ta abata diebainen aerobatōn tropon tina*) for Abaris with his arrow; and on the shaman's drum as equivalent to or replacement for the older bow and arrow, note 10 below. While touching on such matters this is a good point to emphasize that the ability to overcome obstacles is, itself, virtually a definition of Mongolian as well as Siberian shamanism (W. Heissig, *Anthropos* 48, 1953, 507, 510, 516; cf. V. Zikmundová, *Mongolo–Tibetica Pragensia* '08, 1/2, 2008, 166–71, 176). On the Mongols' fondness for making their way against all odds "through inaccessible places" see e.g. T.T. Allsen, *Archivum Eurasiae medii aevi* 7 (1987–91) 12 and 14; Zikmundová 171 n.51; note 33 below. Arrows and ecstasy: Bawden 91-2 n.4 (Mongolia); H.V. Guenther, *The royal song of Saraha* (Berkeley 1973) 5–7 (see below, note 11), T. Ellingson, *Anthropology and humanism* 23 (1998) 51–76 (Tibet); cf. also U. Harva, *Die religiösen Vorstellungen der altaischen Völker* (Helsinki 1938) 555–6 and Eliade, *Shamanism* 227 (Siberia). On the severe problems involved in approaching shamans and understanding the inner dimensions of shamanism see e.g. S. West in *Pontus and the outside world*, ed. C.J. Tuplin (Leiden 2004) 60 with n.49; also D. Ermakov, *Bo and Bön* (Kathmandu 2008) lv–lviii.

10.

On this fundamental shamanic principle see especially the vivid accounts we owe to the extraordinary fieldworker V. Diószegi, *Tracing shamans in Siberia* (Oosterhout 1968) 240–1, 259–62, 320; also U. Harva, *Die religiösen Vorstellungen der altaischen Völker* (Helsinki 1938) 536–9, 543–4; W. Heissig, *Folklore studies* 3 (1944) 45–6 and *The religions of Mongolia* (London 1980) 21–2 (Mongolia); R. de Nebesky-Wojkowitz, *Oracles and demons of Tibet* (The Hague 1956) 542–3 (Tibet). On the drum, described by Diószegi, as a more modern substitute for the older bow and arrow see K. Meuli, *Gesammelte Schriften* (Basel 1975) ii 859 n.4; and for the shaman's drum as, itself, a bow and arrow cf. e.g. L.P. Potapov, *Anthropology of consciousness* 10/4 (1999) 25–6, 30.

Abaris carries his arrow: Herodotus, *Histories* 4.36 (*ton oïston periephere*); Lycurgus fr. 85 Blass = XIV.5 Conomis (cf. C.A. Lobeck, *Aglaophamus*, Königsberg 1829, i 314 n.p). Abaris carried, steered and guided by his arrow past all obstacles: Heraclides Ponticus fr.

51c Wehrli (*epi toutou ... pheromenon*); Origen, *Against Celsus* 3.31 (*oïstōi sumpheresthai*); Iamblichus, *Pythagorean life* 91 (*epochoumenos gar autōi kai ta abata diebainen hoion potamous kai limnas kai telmata kai orē kai ta toiauta*), 136 (*aithrobatēs ... oïstōi ... epochoumenos potamous te kai pelagē kai ta abata diebainen aerobatōn tropon tina*: cf. Porphyry, *Life of Pythagoras* 29), 140-1 (*hēi ekubernato ... hēs aneu ouch hoios t' ēn tas hodous exheuriskein*); Gregory of Nazianzen, *Correspondence with Saint Basil the Great*, Letter 2 (*hupoptere su kai metarsie kai tōi Abaridos oïstōi sumpheromene*: cf. *Sermon* 43.21); Nonnus of Panopolis, *Dionysiaca* 11.132-3 (*... hon eis dromon ēerophoitēn hiptamenōi pompeuen alēmoni Phoibos oïstōi*); Suda s.v. *Abaris* (*... petomenou ...*); above, note 9. J.N. Bremmer (*The rise and fall of the afterlife*, London 2002, 33) agrees with many other scholars in considering it "historically responsible" to suppose that the tradition of Abaris carrying his arrow must be the older and more original one because it already is offered by our earliest source, Herodotus. But responsibility to history involves respecting all the complexities of the evidence, not merely the ones that fit in with our reductive line of approach. And in this case it involves paying attention to three crucial facts. First, Herodotus could hardly be less complete or reliable as a transmitter of ancient sacred and mystical traditions: on the contrary, he is notorious for "drastically rationalizing" figures such as Abaris and being heavily selective in whatever details he does decide to mention (S. West in *Pontus and the outside world*, ed. C.J. Tuplin, Leiden 2004, 48, 58). Second, in this particular case he not only devotes just one very brief and grudging sentence to Abaris but also states quite explicitly that he refuses to waste any more time on the ridiculous stories handed down about him (*ton gar peri Abarios logon tou legomenou einai Huperboreou ou legō*, 4.36; cf. P. Corssen, *Rheinisches Museum* 67, 1912, 46). In short, his decision to remain silent is just as eloquent as the few minimal details he so reluctantly provides. And third, there is the question of Iamblichus' *Pythagorean life* 140-1. For well over a century philologists have noted that the feminine gender of the word "arrow" which occurs twice in this passage points back to Aristotle (*tēn oïston autou apheileto hēi ekubernato ... parelomenos hon eichen oïston chrusoun hēs aneu ouch hoios t' ēn tas hodous exheuriskein*. On the significance of the feminine form see V. Rose, *Aristotelis fragmenta*, Leipzig 1886, 155.8 n.; I. Lévy, *Recherches sur les sources de la légende de Pythagore*, Paris 1926, 16 n.1. For the textual details see A. Nauck, *Iamblichi de vita pythagorica liber*, St. Petersburg 1884, xxvi, lxxiii; L. Deubner, *Bemerkungen zum Text der Vita Pythagorae des Iamblichos*, Berlin 1935, 69). This has led to a strange situation where the passage is often cited (so e.g. W. Burkert, *Lore and science in ancient Pythagoreanism*, Cambridge, MA 1972, 150 n.161; Bremmer 33) as evidence that, according to Aristotle, Abaris carried his arrow rather than being carried by it. But in fact it says nothing of the kind. What the text does show is something quite different, and very important. When we look at Iamblichus' clumsy process of reworking and incorporating Aristotelian material into his narrative, it becomes clear that the details about Pythagoras taking the arrow which Abaris has handed to him—and of this being the arrow that mysteriously steered Abaris on his journey, allowing him to find his way—derive from Aristotle. In other words the issue which has obsessed scholars for so long, as to whether Abaris carries his arrow or is carried by it, was never the real issue at all. The crucial question has always been whether the arrow carried by Abaris in his hand as a token from Apollo is nothing but an inert and passive object or whether it has a magical intelligence (naturally ignored by Herodotus) which allows it to steer, guide and convey Abaris past all obstacles without the slightest resistance just as if he is being carried by it straight through the air. As for the issue of carrying or being carried: the credit for realizing this is a false dilemma goes to Walter Burkert who with rare insight saw it as just a matter of different perspectives, rather than mutually exclusive opposites, and suggested that "the tradition was self-contradictory from the beginning. There were alternative ways to report the activities of the miracle-worker; Abaris could not perhaps 'actually' fly, but he could claim the ability, and even, in ecstatic ritual, act it out, as it were, as a shaman. Whoever was ready in his heart to believe, would speak of 'flying'; those who were ready to discard the old-time magic would report the matter in the style of Herodotus" (*Lore* 150). For a perfect confirmation and demonstration of precisely the point that Burkert is making, see H.P. Duerr, *Dreamtime* (Oxford

1985) 83: "The Sanema Indians told the anthropologist Johannes Wilbert that their shamans could fly, or at least walk one foot above the ground. Naively, the scientist answered that after all, he could *see* that the shamans ran around just like anybody else. Whereupon the Indians countered, 'The reason for that is that you do not *understand*.' And, similarly, a Washo Indian told another anthropologist, 'You have no idea what it is I am talking about, and the same is true of everyone who is going to read that thing that you are just writing'." See also the remarkable descriptions preserved by Diószegi—as referenced at the start of this note—of Siberian shamans flying on and being carried by the instruments that they carry in their hand.

## 11.

For shooting of the magical arrow into the heart compare the famous Tibetan traditions about the arrowmaker's promise to Saraha ("Since this arrow can do anything, I'll shoot it into your heart!": K.R. Schaeffer, *Dreaming the great Brahmin*, New York 2005, 27); and note also the similar notions and forms of expression among Mongol Buryats (B. Adler, *Der Weltkreis* 2, 1931, 102). On the single-pointed focus demanded of both arrowmaker and archer see e.g. H.V. Guenther, *The royal song of Saraha* (Berkeley 1973) 5, Schaeffer 21, 27, and for comments on the spiritual significance of making or shooting arrows cf. also A.K. Coomaraswamy, *What is civilisation?* (Ipswich 1989) 135–56 and *The door in the sky*, ed. R.P. Coomaraswamy (Princeton 1997) 40–1, 100–1, 172, 210–11, 219–29; H.H. Onuma et al., *Kyudo* (Tokyo 1993); S. Ruspoli, *Le livre Tâwasîn de Hallâj* (Beirut 2007) 129–30, 176–7; *Rumi's Sun: the teachings of Shams of Tabriz*, trans. R. Algan and C.A. Helminski (Sandpoint 2008) 55. Skywalking and ecstasy: Guenther 7 with n.8; and note (ibid. 5–7) the close connection between revealing the principles of arrowmaking and providing access to the state of ecstasy. For the essential role of ecstasy in shamanic tradition (occasionally denied by scholars who have not the slightest idea what ecstasy is) cf. e.g. Å. Hultkrantz, *Temenos* 9 (1973) 25–37 and in L. Backman and Hultkrantz, *Studies in Lapp shamanism* (Stockholm

1978) 9–35; A.-L. Siikala's comments in Siikala and M. Hoppál, *Studies on shamanism* (2nd ed., Budapest 1998) 20–1, 26–40; also C. Müller-Ebeling et al., *Shamanism and Tantra in the Himalayas* (Rochester, VT 2002) 38. On the importance not just of entering states of ecstasy but of learning to control and direct them see P. Kingsley, *Reality* (Inverness, CA 2003) 438–53; and for the esoteric principle of inversion according to which appearances are the exact opposite of reality, ibid. 343–461, 588.

**12.**

For Abaris with his arrow as overcomer of obstacles and remover of obstructions cf. Iamblichus, *Pythagorean life* 91 and 136 = Porphyry, *Life of Pythagoras* 29 with notes 9 and 10 above; also Procopius of Gaza, *Letters* 58 (... *ton oïston echōn hupēretounta tēi gnōmēi par' hous ēthelen ēgeto, kai hodou mēkos ouden parelupei ton Abarin*). For Abaris as master of incantations see Plato, *Charmides* 158b–c with M.-F. Hazebroucq, *La folie humaine et ses remèdes* (Paris 1997) 34–5, 128–9; also Iamblichus, *Pythagorean life* 91 (*proslalōn*) with L. Deubner, *Bemerkungen zum Text der Vita Pythagorae des Iamblichos* (Berlin 1935) 65. Abaris as chaser, with his arrow, of epidemics and controller of winds: Iamblichus, *Pythagorean life* 91 (... *katharmous te epetelei kai loimous apediōke kai anemous apo tōn eis touto axiousōn poleōn boēthon auton genesthai*). Abaris talks to his arrow: Iamblichus, *Pythagorean life* 91, where the reading *proslalōn* is correctly defended by Deubner 65 (although his rejection of the less well attested reading *prosbalōn* as "meaningless" is more than a little simplistic). Iamblichus' cautious addition of *hōs logos* straight after *proslalōn*—"And by talking to it, or so we are told"—is a clear sign of his own bewilderment while dutifully repeating what his sources have to say. For Mongol shamans talking to their arrows see e.g. B. Adler, *Der Weltkreis* 2 (1931) 102; H. Göckenjan, *Acta orientalia Academiae Scientiarum Hungaricae* 58 (2005) 61. On the very common link, in Mongolia and elsewhere, between magic arrows and the use of spoken incantations cf. V.M. Mikhailovskii, *Journal of the Anthropological Institute of Great Britain and Ireland* 24 (1895) 96; R. de Nebesky-Wojkowitz, *Oracles and demons of Tibet* (The Hague

1956) 544; J.-P. Roux, *Turcica* 9 (1977) 9; A.K. Coomaraswamy, *The door in the sky*, ed. R.P. Coomaraswamy (Princeton 1997) 172, 211 n.34.

**13.**

The "arrow-circulators" (*chuanjian, chuanjian dahua, chuanjian tonghua*): H. Serruys, *Journal of the American Oriental Society* 78 (1958) 282; and note the survival of analogous traditions among Mongol Buryats which involved shooting, instead of carrying, the arrow (J.G. Georgi, *Russia* iv, London 1783, 148; J. Baldick, *Animal and shaman*, London 2000, 110). Abaris walks with his arrow "in a circle": Lycurgus fr. 85 Blass = XIV.5 Conomis (*enthous genomenos kuklōi periēiei meta belous tēn Hellada* ...); cf. also Herodotus, *Histories* 4.36 (*ton oïston periephere kata pasan gēn), Apollonius, Amazing stories* 4, 122.48 Giannini (*las chōras perierchomenos*). For arrows and circular movement note as well the Indian traditions cited by A.K. Coomaraswamy, *What is civilisation?* (Ipswich 1989) 142. On Abaris staying in sacred places and never being seen eating or drinking cf. Iamblichus, *Pythagorean life* 141 (*katelue de en tois hierois kai oute pinōn oute esthiōn ōphthē pote outhen*); also Herodotus 4.36 (*ouden siteomenos*). In shamanic traditions, neither eating nor drinking is not only a normal by-product of ecstatic states but also a standard way of accessing them (P. Lindegger, *Griechische und römische Quellen zum Peripheren Tibet* i, Rikon 1979, 48 n.4; *Shamanism: critical concepts in sociology* i, ed. A.A. Znamenski, London 2004, xxiv–xxv and 280).

**14.**

On the triple-bladed Avar arrowhead see e.g. W. Pohl, *Die Awaren* (Munich 1988) 170; H. Steuer in *Reallexikon der germanischen Altertumskunde* xvii (2nd ed., Berlin 2004) 79a, 81a, 83a. For the triple-bladed *phurba* and its ancestors cf. esp. G. Meredith, *History of religions* 6 (1967) 237–9; J.C. Huntington, *The* phur-pa (*Artibus Asiae* Supplementum 33, Ascona 1975) vii, 4–5. For use of the *phurba* by Mongols see J. van Durme, *Mélanges chinois et bouddhiques*

1 (1931–32) 296 n.3; W. Heissig, *Folklore studies* 3 (1944) 50; also
C. Müller-Ebeling et al., *Shamanism and Tantra in the Himalayas*
(Rochester, VT 2002) 10 (Mohan Rai); and note the comments in
R. de Nebesky-Wojkowitz, *Oracles and demons of Tibet* (The Hague
1956) 544 about *phurbas* and Buryat shamans. On the shamanic, as
opposed to Indian, origin of *phurbas* see Meredith 237, 246, 250;
Huntington vii, 2–5, 7, 12, 61; K. Dowman, *Sky dancer* (London 1984)
302–3; and for the early examples of *phurbas* found in Khotan or
Chinese Turkestan (between Central Asia, Mongolia and Tibet),
R. Beer, *The encyclopedia of Tibetan symbols and motifs* (Boston 1999)
246. Golden *phurbas*: de Nebesky-Wojkowitz 18, 186, 270, 530;
Meredith 246; Huntington 62, 69; Müller-Ebeling et al. 13. On
*phurbas* working from a distance cf. esp. Huntington vii, 1–2, 4;
also G.W. Schuster, *Das alte Tibet* (St. Pölten 2000) 118–19. On the
ritual interchangeability of *phurba* and arrow see e.g. de Nebesky-
Wojkowitz 317 and 354–5; and note also D. Ermakov, *Bo and Bön*
(Kathmandu 2008) 673. *Phurbas* as "little arrows": Huntington 2,
4 (*saraka*). Flying *phurbas* and shamans riding *phurbas*: Meredith
246, 253; R.A. Paul in *Spirit possession in the Nepal Himalayas*, ed.
J.T. Hitchcock and R.L. Jones (Warminster 1976) 147; Schuster 119;
Müller-Ebeling et al. 10. The *phurba*'s frequent association with
magical flight is strangely overlooked by A. Wayman, *Journal of
the Tibet Society* 1 (1981) 80. *Phurba* as the overcomer of obstacles
and remover of obstructions: Huntington 1–3; cf. also de Nebesky-
Wojkowitz 92 with F.A. Bischoff and C. Hartman in *Études tibétaines
dédiées à la mémoire de Marcelle Lalou* (Paris 1971) 19 and 23 §8. For
*phurbas* and incantations see e.g. Meredith 245–7, 253; Huntington
5, 12. Used to chase diseases and epidemics, and control the spirits
of the weather and winds: Meredith 245–9; Huntington 4–5, 8; Beer
247; Schuster 95–8 (cf. de Nebesky-Wojkowitz 471); note also S.G.
Karmay, *Secret visions of the Fifth Dalai Lama* (Chicago 1998) 15, 30;
and on spirits as the cause of epidemics see Heissig as quoted in
note 8 above. The primordial *phurba* at Sera monastery: Meredith
246; see also Schuster 96–7. The modern shaman of Mongol ancestry:
Müller-Ebeling et al. 10 (Mohan Rai); and cf. Schuster 118–19.
This total merging of *phurba* and shaman helps to place in proper
perspective the pointless attempts by western scholars (see e.g. F.

Lefherz, *Studien zu Gregor von Nazianz*, Bonn 1958, 57) to decide whether Abaris' magical power of flight belonged to him or to his arrow. Cf. also J.-P. Roux, *Turcica* 9 (1977) 9, 12, on the Central Asiatic traditions of arrow as shaman and shaman as arrow, with e.g. L.P. Lhalungpa, *The life of Milarepa* (Boulder 1984) 178.

**15.**

The best remaining account of these practices, predictably often dismissed by those unfamiliar with Tibetan traditions, is Alexandra David-Neel's: *With mystics and magicians in Tibet* (London 1931) 199–216. Cf. also W.Y. Evans-Wentz, *The Tibetan book of the great liberation* (Oxford 1954) 137, 166–7 n. 4; Lama Anagarika Govinda, *The way of the white clouds* (London 1966) 80–2; L.P. Lhalungpa, *The life of Milarepa* (Boulder 1984) 4, 100 with n.10, 129, 178; G.W. Schuster, *Das alte Tibet* (St. Pölten 2000) 188–98; E.R. Gruber, *Aus dem Herzen Tibets* (Frankfurt 2007) 251–2, where the contemporary autobiographical report by Chetsang Rinpoche contains a reference to the same practices; and the further comments in note 16 below. For priests of Apollo, movement and breath control, stillness and calm, see P. Kingsley, *In the dark places of wisdom* (Inverness, CA 1999), esp. 106–115, and *Reality* (Inverness, CA 2003).

These traditional practices of ecstatic walking naturally throw light on the reports about Aristeas, "seized by Apollo," traveling into Central Asia in a state of ecstasy (above, note 2). They also offer a very welcome corrective to the thinking of western scholars who, crippled by rationalistic and Christian dualisms, assume without hesitation that anyone engaging in "ecstatic travel" must be doing so purely on the level of the soul after leaving the gross physical body behind (so e.g. P. Hadot, *What is ancient philosophy?*, Cambridge, MA 2002, 184–5)—and who enjoy pointing out, with studied mockery, that anyone foolish enough to try traveling physically while in a state of ecstasy is of course never going to get very far (K. Dowden, *Revue des études grecques* 93, 1980, 491). It can be quite staggering to see how people with such limited horizons feel able to write about religious and spiritual experience.

**16.**

For some general comments on this sacred Tibetan ritual, and the preparations involved, see A. David-Neel's *With mystics and magicians in Tibet* (London 1931) 204–9; also R. de Nebesky-Wojkowitz, *Oracles and demons of Tibet* (The Hague 1956) 533–7; G.W. Schuster, *Das alte Tibet* (St. Pölten 2000) 191–6; and note Chetsang Rinpoche's eye-witness description of one preparatory exercise as recorded in E.R. Gruber, *Aus dem Herzen Tibets* (Frankfurt 2007) 91–3. De Nebesky-Wojkowitz's delightfully Herodotean account is striking not only for its factual inaccuracy but, above all, for its reasonable absurdity. In particular there is no way that the moderately strenuous walk he tries to portray would have demanded eleven years of the most intense esoteric training, or called for months of rest after the circuit was complete. I owe the fondest gratitude to Lobsang Lhalungpa—former secretary to His Holiness the Fourteenth Dalai Lama at the Potala palace in Lhasa, and son of the greatest official oracle in Tibet—for his intimate recollections of the traditional training undergone by these future wind walkers at centers such as the famous monasteries (cf. David-Neel 205, de Nebesky-Wojkowitz 533) of Tsang province.

**17.**

On the history of the *phurba* see above, note 14. As for the wider issue of shamanic influence on the traditions of Tibetan and Mongolian Buddhism—an issue which has been very much obscured not only by Tibetan Buddhists' outward stance of dismissing shamanism as "irreligious," but also by their systematic persecution and extermination of indigenous shamans over the centuries (below, note 24)—cf. e.g. R. de Nebesky-Wojkowitz, *Oracles and demons of Tibet* (The Hague 1956) 538–53; M. Eliade, *History of religions* 1 (1961) 165–7, 176–8; R.A. Paul in *Spirit possession in the Nepal Himalayas*, ed. J.T. Hitchcock and R.L. Jones (Warminster 1976) 141–51; B.N. Aziz, ibid. 343–60; W.G. Stablein, ibid. 361–75; W. Heissig, *The religions of Mongolia* (London 1980) 11–12, 36–45; F. Pommaret, *Les revenants de l'au-delà dans le monde tibétain* (Paris 1989) 153–61 with P. Gignoux, *Les inscriptions de Kirdīr et sa vision de l'au-delà* (Rome 1990); S.B. Ortner, *Ethos* 23 (1995) 381–2; R.A. Ray, *Journal of religion* 75 (1995) 98–9; O. Purev and G. Purvee, *Mongolian shamanism* (Ulaanbaatar 2004) 65; J.V. Bellezza, *Spirit-mediums, sacred mountains and related Bon textual traditions in Upper Tibet* (Leiden 2005) 20–52. There can be no taking seriously Geoffrey Samuel's idea (*Tantric revisionings*, Farnham 2005) that whatever shamanic elements survived in Tibetan Buddhism derive from India: this notion relies on a metaphorical use of the word "shaman" which strips it of any real sense, on an Indocentrism more appropriate to the days of the Raj, and on the magical ability of some modern scholars to make all traces of pre-Buddhist Tibetan shamanism simply disappear.

**18.**
Abaris hands over his arrow: Iamblichus, *Pythagorean life* 91–2, 140–1. Recent scholars have rightly drawn attention to the antiquity of this episode and noted that it at least predates Aristotle (cf. e.g. W. Burkert, *Lore and science in ancient Pythagoreanism*, Cambridge, MA 1972, 143 n.127 and 150 with note 10 above; B.L. van der Waerden, *Die Pythagoreer*, Zurich 1979, 59, 90–3; B. Centrone in *Dictionnaire des philosophes antiques* i, ed. R. Goulet, Paris 1989, 45). For the detailed description at 91–2 of the hand-over as an essential ingredient in the formal process of establishing a solemn and intimate relationship of mutual trust between Abaris and Pythagoras (... *pisteusas ... pistin hikanēn paraschōn* ...), see A.P.D. Mourelatos' comments on the formalities and exchange of pledges involved in a relationship of mutual trust or *pistis*: *The route of Parmenides* (2nd ed., Las Vegas 2008) 136-44. The Mongol custom: cf. e.g. H. Serruys, *Journal of the American Oriental Society* 78 (1958) 279, 284; Hok-Lam Chan, *Asia Major* 4/2 (1991) 55. Altan Khan: Serruys 284; and for his encounter with the Dalai Lama see note 24 below. On arrows as tokens cf. also the references in notes 6 and 7 above.

**19.**

For the unending uncertainties in the West over whether Pythagoras deprived Abaris of his arrow or Abaris just meekly handed it to Pythagoras see Iamblichus, *Pythagorean life* 91–2 (*apedōken*) and 140–1 (*apheileto ... parhelomenos*); P. Corssen, *Rheinisches Museum* 67 (1912) 38; I. Lévy, *Recherches sur les sources de la légende de Pythagore* (Paris 1926) 13-19; B. Einarson, *Classical philology* 51 (1956) 177; W. Burkert, *Lore and science in ancient Pythagoreanism* (Cambridge, MA 1972) 143 n.127; J.M. Dillon and J.P. Hershbell, *Iamblichus on the Pythagorean way of life* (Atlanta 1991) 115 n.3. On the ways in which Abaris was eventually chewed up by the Pythagorean propaganda machine and converted into the prime exhibit for Pythagoreanism's effectiveness as a teaching system, see Iamblichus 90–3. This is part and parcel of the policy that made him, just like Empedocles and Epimenides, "receive" all his powers from Pythagoras (ibid. 135 = Porphyry, *Life of Pythagoras* 29: the common translation of *metalabontas* as "sharing" may be far more diplomatic, but is not correct) and turned him into one of Pythagoras' disciples (Iamblichus 267; but contrast the scholia to Plato's *Republic* 600b, and the *Suda* s.v. *Puthagoras*, where Pythagoras has become the disciple of Abaris). The dogma that "whatever the Greeks receive from barbarians they improve on and carry to perfection"—and that Athenians are the most perfect among the perfect—is nowhere articulated more forcefully than by Platonists at Athens (cf. *Epinomis* 987d–988a; P. Kingsley, *Journal of the Royal Asiatic Society* 5, 1995, 200 n.171; below, note 23). This is obviously relevant to the crude Athenocentrism which has contaminated surviving traditions about Abaris (for Lycurgus see S.C. Humphreys, *The strangeness of gods*, Oxford 2004, 103, with T.P. Bridgman, *Hyperboreans*, New York 2005, 66); but we also are able to be more specific. There can be little doubt (cf. F. Wehrli, *Herakleides Pontikos*, 2nd ed., Basel 1969, 84–6) that the familiar stories about Abaris' encounter with Pythagoras have passed through the hands of Heraclides Ponticus, a close friend of Plato and a prominent figure in the early Platonic Academy, although we have no reason to suppose he did much more than clumsily tinker with and embellish some of their most superficial details. Scholars have had solid grounds for supposing that those stories must be older than him (Burkert 103 n.32); already in his own lifetime he had as big a reputation for plagiarism as for any genuinely creative thought (fr. 176 with Wehrli ad loc.); and there are significant cases where the basic elements in Heraclides' apparent works of fiction have been shown either to derive from earlier sources or to be accurate reflections of historical fact (cf. e.g. P. Kingsley, *Journal of the Royal Asiatic Society* 5, 1995, 187–9 with the references in n.102; *Ancient philosophy, mystery and magic*, Oxford 1995, 234–7, 256; and see also note 10 above for the legend of Abaris flying on his arrow, which some modern scholars have misguidedly dismissed as no more than Heraclides' fanciful invention). Even more importantly, it should be added that Heraclides had a unique knack not only for misunderstanding those older traditions and symbols and themes he tried to retouch but also for getting everything back to front through his tendency to oversimplify and trivialize and "rationalize the obscure, with the common result of giving motifs, symbols, or ritual practices a meaning the very opposite of the significance they would seem originally to have had" (Kingsley, *Ancient philosophy* 236–7). And to end with just one detail: the portrait preserved by Iamblichus of Abaris as an "old man" or *presbutēs* (*Pythagorean life* 90–1), so implausible in the case of someone needing so much energy to travel so far, must have resulted from mishearing or misreading the original description of Abaris as an "ambassador" or *presbeutēs* (above, note 7)—in much the same way that the original description of Abaris coming to Greece as an "envoy" ended up mistakenly being changed, thanks to misunderstanding of a single word, into the quite different portrayal of him visiting Greece as just a curious spectator (*elthonta theōron eis tēn Hellada*: scholia to Aristophanes' *Knights* 729a Mervyn Jones–Wilson, cf. note 7 above; *elthonta epi historiai tēs Hellados*: ibid. 729d, missing the technical sense of *theōron*). But there happens to be more to the matter than that. The reduction of Abaris to an old man or *presbutēs*, very much out of his element and forced into the shadows by the overwhelming presence of Pythagoras, is formally identical to Plato's fictitious reduction of Parmenides to an old man or *presbutēs*, himself portrayed as very much out of his element in Athens and thrown into the

115

shadows by the overwhelming presence of Socrates (*Parmenides* 127b; Kingsley, *In the dark places of wisdom*, Inverness, CA 1999, 39–40). This could hardly be less surprising: we happen to know that to imitate memorable features of the settings Plato created for his fictional dialogues, and then use them to give a new spin to those ancient traditions he decided to play around with on his own, was a favorite trick of Heraclides Ponticus (Kingsley, *Ancient philosophy* 235 n.11). But even that trickery, that manipulation of history, was by no means an innovation on the part of Heraclides himself. For Plato's own altering of facts and distorting of motives in his imaginary portrayal of Parmenides arriving at Athens see Kingsley, *Dark places* 36–45, 199–203. And for the many problems caused by Plato's, as well as his successors', conscious rationalizings and unconscious misunderstandings of older Pythagorean practices or themes cf. Kingsley, *Ancient philosophy* and *Dark places*, esp. 69, 90–1, 158–62, 196–202, 207–13.

## 20.

What Abaris saw and knew in advance: Iamblichus, *Pythagorean life* 91–2, 135. The connection between the two themes of Abaris handing over his arrow—which aside from being confirmed by Mongol traditions is clearly ancient (above, note 18)—and of him acknowledging Pythagoras' exceptional status is so seamless, as well as being strengthened even further by the archaic element of mutual *pistis* or trust (ibid.), that this second theme too must be very old. Pythagoras already is referred to by Aristotle (fr. 191 Rose) as an incarnation of Apollo. It will be noted how striking the contrast is in our sources between Abaris and the other people around Pythagoras: Abaris inwardly recognized that Pythagoras was an incarnation of Apollo while everyone else just repeated the rumor (cf. e.g. Aristotle, loc. cit., 154.24–5 *doxan eichon peri autou*). For Abaris' direct insight into Pythagoras' real nature see also J.Z. Smith's comments, *Map is not territory* (Leiden 1978) 203.

On Apollo's decision to take physical form (*anthrōpomorphos*) as Pythagoras for the benefit of incarnate beings see Iamblichus, *Pythagorean life* 92, where the emphasis is placed on Apollo's compassionate wish to help heal and be of service to incarnate humans. But the wish to help and be of service to other, non-human, sentient beings is given equal emphasis in ancient accounts about Pythagoras. For the extraordinary teaching, and enduring personal example, of compassion towards animals that he introduced into the western world cf. e.g. A. Schopenhauer, *The basis of morality*, trans. A.B. Bullock (2nd ed., London 1915) 223; W. Tuttle, *The world peace diet* (Brooklyn, NY 2005) 24–5; C.L. Joost-Gaugier, *Measuring heaven* (Ithaca, NY 2006) 12, 246. On later Greek traditions about Pythagoras' compassionate act of incarnating as a human, and their intimate link with Sufi notions of the *quṭb* or "Pole," see D.J. O'Meara, *Pythagoras revived* (Oxford 1989) 36–9 with P. Kingsley, *Ancient philosophy, mystery and magic* (Oxford 1995) 380–3; and on their striking similarity to the *bodhisattva* figure in Buddhism cf. G. Shaw's comments, *Theurgy and the soul* (University Park, PA 1995) 144 n.1, 116 n.6, 151. Also a part of the same pattern is the selflessness of Pythagoras' earlier incarnation, Hermotimus, in acting as a messenger on behalf of other humans who have no direct access to the divine (J.D.P. Bolton, *Aristeas of Proconnesus*, Oxford 1962, 121, 128, 148–9; P. Kingsley, *Reality*, Inverness, CA 2003, 563 with note 22 below). The appalling lack of attention as well as respect which has been shown toward the elements of compassion and selflessness in ancient Greek philosophy is partly due to the insistence of early Christians on trivializing the historical evidence for their own polemical purposes, and partly due to the intellectual self-indulgence of modern academics who are too lazy to question the results of that trivializing.

As the best scholars have come to realize, there is nothing at all accidental about the fact that our earliest evidence in the West for ideas relating to reincarnation points to the outermost and easternmost edges of the Greek world (cf. esp. W. Burkert, *Kleine Schriften* iii, Göttingen 2006, 56–7, 204). There also can be no doubting the importance of detailed parallels between some of these ancient Greek ideas and several themes we find embedded in Indian literature: see e.g. M.L. West, *Early Greek philosophy and the Orient* (Oxford 1971) 62–3; also T. McEvilley, *The shape of ancient thought* (New York 2002) 98–143, although McEvilley's grasp of

the Greek material is poor and his dating of non-Greek traditions
highly unreliable (J. Bussanich, *International journal of Hindu studies*
9, 2005, 4). And very naturally there is a significance in the fact
that Pythagoras—with his reputation for being the first westerner
to speak out openly on the topic of incarnating and reincarnating
(Dicaearchus in Porphyry's *Life of Pythagoras* 19; Kingsley, *Ancient
philosophy* 366–9)—also happened to be a legend for his extensive
travels outside of Greece. See below, notes 26–27.

"Both from the noble marks he observed in him …": Iamblichus,
*Pythagorean life* 91 (*ek te hōn heōra peri auton semnōmatōn kai ex hōn
proeginōsken hōs hiereus gnōrismatōn*). The word *semnōmata*, in this
context meaning visibly "noble marks" or "noble characteristics,"
is as remarkable as it happens to be unusual. For the importance
attached to observing the "noble marks" or "noble characteristics"
of a great being—among pre-Buddhist Indian Brahmins, in the
earliest of Buddhist texts, and through into the mainstream of
Tibetan Buddhist tradition—see e.g. Har Dayal, *The bodhisattva
doctrine in Buddhist Sanskrit literature* (London 1932) 305 with P.G.
Jestice, *Holy people of the world* (Santa Barbara 2004) 79; *The Sutta-
Nipāta*, trans. H. Saddhatissa (London 1985) 46 §§408–410; Prem
Singh Jina, *Recent researches on the Himalaya* (New Delhi 1997) 93.
For the formalities associated with being shown in advance the
tokens or proofs of identity that will allow a *tulku* to be found
and recognized and announced (coupled, in due course, with
direct observation of the noble characteristics) cf. Tenzin Gyatso,
*Freedom in exile* (London 1990) 11–12, 215–17; C. Allen, *The search
for Shangri-La* (London 1999) 21; A. Norman in *The Dalai Lamas*,
ed. M. Brauen (Chicago 2005) 163. Regarding the *tulku* institution,
which for centuries has been of such central importance in both
Tibetan and Mongolian Buddhism, see Tenzin Gyatso 10–13, 215–18;
Chögyam Trungpa, *Born in Tibet* (3rd ed., Boston 1995) 270–1 = *The
collected works of Chögyam Trungpa* i (Boston 2003) 288–9; P. Logan,
*Harvard Asia Quarterly* 8/1 (2004) 15–23; L.W.J. van der Kuijp in
*The Dalai Lamas*, ed. M. Brauen (Chicago 2005) 15–29; and for its
history and origins, note 24 below.

## 21.

For Apollo as the most Greek of the gods see e.g. W. Burkert, *Greek religion* (Oxford 1985) 143; E.L. Brown in *Charis. Essays in honor of Sara A. Immerwahr*, ed. A.P. Chapin (Princeton 2004) 243. On his fundamental affinities with ecstasy and riddles, incantations and darkness and night, cf. P. Kingsley, *In the dark places of wisdom* (Inverness, CA 1999) esp. 87–92, *Ancient philosophy* 22 (2002) 369–81, and *Reality* (Inverness, CA 2003). And for the ancient logic linking the sun, as well as Apollo, with the underworld and the depths of blackness see also Kingsley, *Ancient philosophy, mystery and magic* (Oxford 1995) 49–68. For Apollo's terrifying destructiveness cf. M. Vogel, *Rheinisches Museum* 107 (1964) 36 with n.10; H. Kothe, *Klio* 52 (1970) 206–7; M. Detienne, *Apollon le couteau à la main* (Paris 1998); Kingsley, *Dark places* 57, 91. Apollo's shrines and the speaking of strange languages: see *Homeric hymn to Apollo* 160–4 (where *bambaliastun* at 162 is clearly the correct reading and should be spared the quaint rationalizations it has been subjected to) together with Herodotus, *Histories* 4.35; Pausanias, *Description of Greece* 10.5.7–8; U. von Wilamowitz-Moellendorff, *Die Ilias und Homer* (Berlin 1916) 450–2; F. Cassola, *Inni omerici* (Milan 1975) 497; R. Viard, *Revue de philologie* 79 (2005) 123–49; and, for the case of Apollo's oracle at Didyma, F. Graf, *Apollo* (London 2006) 81 with Kingsley, *Dark places* 88. On Apollo's constant remoteness, and quality of coming from far away, cf. H.S. Versnel, *Transition and reversal in myth and ritual* (2nd ed., Leiden 1994) 303 with n.47. For the Greek tradition—rightly described by classicists as "quite bizarre" (A.G. Keen, *Dynastic Lycia*, Leiden 1998, 198)—that Leto gave birth to Apollo after arriving from Hyperborea in the form of a wolf accompanied by other wolves see T.P. Bridgman, *Hyperboreans* (New York 2005) 69-70 with Graf 99. On the importance of wolf origins among the Mongols and in Central Asia cf. *The secret history of the Mongols* §1, trans. P. Kahn and F.W. Cleaves (2nd ed., Boston 1998) 3; M. Eliade, *Zalmoxis, the vanishing god* (Chicago 1972) 1–20; D. Sinor in *Folklorica: Festschrift for Felix J. Oinas*, ed. E.V. Zygas and P. Voorheis (Bloomington 1982) 223–57; J. Weatherford, *Genghis Khan and the making of the modern world* (New York 2004) 9, 65–6; P.B. Golden in *A tribute to Omeljan Pritsak*, ed. M. Alpargu and Y. Öztürk (Sakarya 2007) 149–65; D. Ermakov, *Bo and Bön* (Kathmandu 2008) 70, 80. For Apollo's non-Greek origins see e.g. W.K.C. Guthrie, *The Greeks and their gods* (London 1950) 82–7, 204; Kothe 205–14; G. Ashe, *The ancient wisdom* (London 1977) 98–102; D. Hegyi, *Acta antiqua Academiae Scientiarum Hungaricae* 32 (1989) 5–21; R.S.P. Beekes, *Journal of ancient Near Eastern religions* 3 (2003) 1–21; Brown 243–57. On the Hyperborean ancestry of Apollo's most famous shrines and Greece's most sacred institutions, as well as the strains and tensions this gave rise to, see J.S. Romm, *The edges of the earth in ancient thought* (Princeton 1992) 60–7; Pindar (*Pythian odes* 10.34–5) was not alone in portraying Apollo as far happier among the Hyperboreans than anywhere else. For the destruction of the original Pythagorean bases in Italy cf. e.g. J.S. Morrison, *Classical quarterly* 6 (1956) 146–8; W. Burkert, *Lore and science in ancient Pythagoreanism* (Cambridge, MA 1972) 115–20; C. Riedweg, *Pythagoras* (Ithaca, NY 2005) 100–6.

Pythagoras as "Hyperborean Apollo": Aristotle fr. 191 Rose = Aelian, *Historical miscellany* 2.26 (*Apollōna Huperboreion*) and Iamblichus, *Pythagorean life* 140 (*Apollōna Huperboreon*). Iamblichus also calls him "the Apollo from Hyperborea" (*ton ex Huperboreōn Apollōna*: ibid. 30 = Aristotle fr. 192); "the Apollo there," referring to the land of the Hyperboreans (*elthe men gar Abaris apo Huperboreōn, hiereus tou ekei Apollōnos ... kai malista eikasas tōi theōi houper ēn hiereus*: ibid. 91); and "the Apollo in Hyperborea" (*... Apollōna einai ton en Huperboreois, houper ēn hiereus ho Abaris ... tou en Huperboreois Apollōnos*: ibid. 135–6 = Porphyry, *Life of Pythagoras* 28–9). Sadly, scholars treat these expressions with complete casualness as though they were commonplaces in the ancient Greek world (so e.g. E.R. Dodds, *The Greeks and the irrational*, Berkeley 1956, 141, 161 n.36). But in fact there is no chance of even beginning to assess their significance until we notice that they never once occur, anywhere, outside of an immediate reference to either Abaris or Pythagoras. To say, as Greeks often did, that Apollo loved traveling to Hyperborea and was well received by the people there is one thing; to describe Apollo as, himself, a Hyperborean is quite another matter. It will be noted that the alternative way of referring to Pythagoras' true self—as "Apollo arrived from Hyperborea"

(*Apollōn ex Huperboreōn aphigmenos*: Diogenes Laertius, *Lives and views of famous philosophers* 8.11 = Aristotle fr. 191; cf. Iamblichus 30 = Aristotle fr. 192)—further underscores his connection with Abaris (see Harpocration s.v. *Abaris: ex Huperboreōn ... aphikesthai*, etc.). This, in turn, helps give due emphasis to the very telling fact that "Hyperborean Abaris" and the elusive expression "Hyperborean Apollo" happen to be so closely and explicitly linked in our sources (Iamblichus 135 = Porphyry 28). Also worth noting is the strange logic that has Pythagoras, as a demonstrable "proof" of being the Hyperborean Apollo, show Abaris his thigh which is made of gold (Iamblichus 92, and 135 = Porphyry 28). Pythagoras' notorious golden thigh has already been connected with shamanic traditions and rituals of death, dismemberment and rebirth (W. Burkert, *Kleine Schriften* viii, Göttingen 2008, 20–3 and *Lore* 159–60; Kingsley, *Ancient philosophy, mystery and magic* 291). But what still remains to be pointed out is just how common and widespread the ritual practice of dismemberment—plus the replacing of body parts with substitute pieces, often made of gold—used to be beyond the Altai mountains in the regions of Mongolia, Siberia and Tibet (Chu Junjie in *Theses on Tibetology in China*, ed. Hu Tan, Beijing 1991, 133; V.A. Semyonov in *Tsentralnaya Aziya i Pribaykalye v drevosti*, ed. M.V. Konstantinov and A.D. Tsybiktarov, Ulan-Ude 2002, 88–92; J.V. Bellezza, *Zhang Zhung*, Vienna 2008, 556–7).

On Pythagoras' reputation for speaking in riddles see e.g. Iamblichus 161; Kingsley, *Ancient philosophy, mystery and magic* 38, 43 n.26, 330 with n.47, 363 with n.12, 366 n.20, 375–6 with n.14; A. Berra in *Texts of power, the power of the text*, ed. C. Galewicz (Kraków 2006) 259–72. On Pythagoras as originator of the word "philosophy" cf. B.L. van der Waerden, *Die Pythagoreer* (Zurich 1979) 194, 298, 309; Kingsley, *Ancient philosophy, mystery and magic* 339 with n.14 and *Dark places* 224 with the further references at 254; C. Riedweg in *Antike Literatur in neuer Deutung. Festschrift für Joachim Latacz*, ed. A. Bierl et al. (Munich 2004) 147–81; L. Gemelli Marciano, *Die Vorsokratiker* i (Düsseldorf 2007) 203–4, 412–14, 423. For the mutual understanding and recognition between Pythagoras and Abaris as the recognition and understanding of like by like, see J.Z. Smith's comments in *Map is not territory* (Leiden 1978) 203; and for similar observations on the Tibetan process of identifying and recognizing *tulkus* cf. P. Moran, *Buddhism observed* (London 2004) 16–17 ("When it comes to reading the signs that announce a tulku's presence ... if there seems to be one rule about the recognition process, it is quite simply that high-ranking emanations are able to recognize their own; they see special qualities with special eyes").

**22.**
On the early history of the trade network, connecting China to Central Asia and Europe, which later would come to be known as the Silk Road see note 27 below. Hermotimus as shaman: F.A. Carus, *Geschichte der Psychologie = Nachgelassene Werke* iii (Leipzig 1808) 212; E.B. Tylor, *Primitive culture* (1st ed., London 1871) i 396–7 (= 6th ed., London 1920, i 439); A. Bastian, *Der Buddhismus in seiner Psychologie* (Berlin 1882) vi–vii and *Die mikronesischen Colonien aus ethnologischen Gesichtspunkten* (Berlin 1899) 55–6; K. Gaiser in *Aristoteles: Werk und Wirkung, Paul Moraux gewidmet*, ed. J. Wiesner (Berlin 1985) 479–80; F. Graf, *Nordionische Kulte* (Rome 1985) 390 with the references in n.57, 392. For the very familiar phenomenon of shamans lying motionless on the ground while traveling invisibly to other worlds see esp. E. Lot-Falck, *Asie du sud-est et monde insulindien* 4/3 (1973) 9 and e.g. Tylor, loc. cit.; V. Diószegi, *Acta ethnographica Academiae Scientiarum Hungaricae* 7 (1958) 97–135; P. Lindegger, *Griechische und römische Quellen zum Peripheren Tibet* i (Rikon 1979) 48 n.4; B. Dumoulin, *Recherches sur le premier Aristote* (Paris 1981) 92; P. Gignoux, *Les inscriptions de Kirdīr et sa vision de l'au-delà* (Rome 1990) 9–19. Pliny's plain and unmistakable reference to Hermotimus' practice of bringing back from his journeys "many messages" (*multa adnuntiare*: *Natural history* 7.174) implies, without any ambiguity, that Hermotimus was offering a service to his community; and, it should be added, the way Pliny goes straight on to describe how people from a hostile religious group ended up burning his body and killing him also implies Hermotimus made enemies because of the service he provided. This shows the utter foolishness of arguments by modern scholars that there can be no such phenomenon as an ancient Greek shamanism because

traditional shamans "undertake their soul journeys on behalf of the community, and on their return bring back a message for the community. We find nothing even remotely similar among the so-called Greek 'shamans': their soul journeys are a purely private affair and there is never the slightest mention of any message. Nothing could demonstrate more forcefully that we need to emphasize the difference, not the similarities, between northern shamans and Greek figures such as Aristeas or Hermotimus" (C.J. de Vogel, *Philosophia* i, Assen 1970, 103, repeating J.A. Philip, *Pythagoras and early Pythagoreanism*, Toronto 1966, 159–61; for Aristeas bringing back news and messages from his journeys see Origen, *Against Celsus* 3.26 with J.D.P. Bolton, *Aristeas of Proconnesus*, Oxford 1962, 128). On the other equally grotesque and groundless arguments which have been put forward against the existence of a Greek shamanic phenomenon see P. Kingsley, *Studia Iranica* 23 (1994) 187–98; and on the general theme of bringing back messages from another world, *Reality* (Inverness, CA 2003) 563 with note 20 above. E. Rohde originally pointed to Indian traditions as relevant parallels for the story of Hermotimus being killed while out of his body (*Rheinisches Museum* 26, 1871, 558–9 n.), but later he recanted and regretted suggesting "any historical connexion" (*Psyche*, London 1925, 331 n.112). There are academics who still are fond of giving Hermotimus labels such as "frantic eccentric" (G. Betegh, *The Derveni papyrus*, Cambridge 2004, 285)—a breathtakingly inappropriate designation for someone so experienced in utter stillness. On western scholars' congenital inability to come to grips with the realities of physical and mental stillness see P. Kingsley, *In the dark places of wisdom* (Inverness, CA 1999) and *Reality* 150–6. And then there are those academics who feel they can dismiss Hermotimus as "a purely legendary figure" with no possible historical or philosophical significance (H. Cherniss, *Aristotle's criticism of Presocratic philosophy*, Baltimore 1935, 222 n.20): it is fascinating to watch the finesse with which narrowly rationalizing scholars dispose of whatever they despise and disapprove of. As for the idea, revived by J.N. Bremmer (*The rise and fall of the afterlife*, London 2002, 38–9), that Hermotimus' ecstatic journeys are just a fantastic invention by Heraclides Ponticus: this is indefensible for any number of literary as well as historical reasons (cf. e.g. R.J. Clark, *Transactions and proceedings of the American Philological Association* 99, 1968, 66 n.12; Graf, *Nordionische Kulte* 390–5). The popular trick of discrediting evidence for ancient Greek mystical traditions as nothing more than the products of Heraclides' over-imaginative and romantic brain, aside from being contradicted by the facts (see above, note 19; below, note 23), is at bottom just another pseudo-scholarly ruse for cleansing western history of its most enigmatic and less-than-rational elements. On the profound irrationality of this purging process, and its devastating results, see P. Kingsley, *Ancient philosophy* 22 (2002) 354–6.

Hermotimus and the history of consciousness: Aristotle, *Metaphysics* 984b15–20 and fr. 61 Rose = Iamblichus, *Protrepticus* 48.9–18 Pistelli; F.A. Carus, *Ideen zur Geschichte der Philosophie = Nachgelassene Werke* iv (Leipzig 1809) 330–92; M. Detienne, *Revue philosophique de la France et de l'étranger* 89 (1964) 167–78; Betegh 283–5. In connection with Hermotimus, the faculty of *nous* means pure consciousness or awareness as opposed to the infinitely feebler faculty of thinking which is unable to exist independent of the body: for this original meaning of the word see Kingsley, *Reality* 77–82. The fact that later thinkers (e.g. Aristotle, fr. 61 Rose) mistakenly understood it as referring to the faculty of ordinary intellect or thought—which is the only thing they, as intellectuals, were able to relate to—has been one of the greatest absurdities, and tragedies, in the history of western culture. See also *Reality* 514–17.

## 23.

Hermotimus identifies what belonged to him, as Euphorbus, in his previous incarnation: Diogenes Laertius, *Lives and views of famous philosophers* 8.4–5 = Heraclides Ponticus fr. 89 Wehrli (... *epeidē de Euphorbos apothanoi, metabēnai tēn psuchēn autou eis Hermotimon, hos kai autos pistin thelōn dounai epanēlthen eis Branchidas kai eiselthōn eis to tou Apollōnos hieron epedeixen hēn Menelaos anethēken aspida: ephē gar auton hot' apeplei ek Troias anatheinai tōi Apollōni tēn aspida diasesēpuian ēdē, monon de diamenein to elephantinon prosōpon ...*). For the reappearance of the word *pistis* here see above, notes 18 and

20; and for reactions by Christian fathers to those stories about the recognition scene which had become popular knowledge in their time see Tertullian, *On the soul* 28, 31 (cf. also Lactantius, *Divine institutions* 3.18); M. Peris, *Sri Lanka journal of the humanities* 14 (1988) 75–77, 81–2, 89–90.

Later sources than Heraclides replace this dramatic scenario, of Hermotimus identifying the shield that used to belong to him in his previous incarnation, with an alternative one of Pythagoras being the person who identifies the shield that had belonged to an incarnation of his many centuries earlier; and modern scholars, above all Walter Burkert (*Lore and science in ancient Pythagoreanism*, Cambridge, MA 1972, 138–41), have tried to find reasons for preferring this later version. But their arguments, aside from having no force, depend on overlooking the most important factors. First of all, the general process of devout Pythagoreans transferring to Pythagoras himself the credit for feats originally performed by others somehow associated with him—whether Hermotimus, Abaris or Empedocles—is not only as predictable as the law of gravity. It also is very well attested (see above, note 19). The logic behind a transfer of the recognition scene from Hermotimus to Pythagoras is completely understandable, and extremely easy to find parallels for; on the other hand, there was no rationale at all for transferring it from Pythagoras to Hermotimus. Already we can see that nothing could be more topsy-turvy or back-to-front than to accuse Heraclides, who is our earliest source for the story, of "trapping himself in the awkward situation of having to make Hermotimus instead of Pythagoras prove his identity with Euphorbus" (F. Wehrli, *Herakleides Pontikos*, 2nd ed., Basel 1969, 90). Secondly: Burkert's influential argument that the original form of the Pythagoras legend would have given him just one earlier incarnation (Euphorbus, *Lore* 140), because this would have been the only one needed to bridge the gap between his own period and the Homeric age, is not only more than a little simplistic but exceptionally wide of the mark. The phenomenon of rebirth is founded on the principle of sequential continuity, not dualistic singularity, as we can see with perfect clarity from the early Greek evidence (see e.g. Empedocles frs. 117 and 129.5–6 Diels–Kranz with A. Delatte, *La vie de Pythagore de Diogène Laërce*, Brussels 1922, 155–7; P. Kingsley, *Ancient philosophy* 22, 2002, 355 and 401 with n.167). Thirdly, the list of Pythagoras' earlier embodiments offered by Dicaearchus and Clearchus is not an alternative tradition (as claimed by Burkert, *Lore* 138–9) but is based on what we find in Heraclides: cf. M. Peris, *University of Ceylon review* 21, 1963, 198, together with Burkert himself (139) on the "beautiful prostitute" as just "a sarcastic addition of Dicaearchus." Fourthly: the idea that Heraclides Ponticus was a creative inventor of stories about Pythagoras or related figures, rather than just a sometimes unintelligent transmitter and garbler of earlier traditions about them, is itself no more than a modern myth (see above, notes 19 and 22). In fact it happens to be only one small cog in the much larger myth according to which, with the passing of time, originally very simple traditions about Pythagoras became more and more fantastic and ornate thanks to the inventiveness of subsequent writers (see e.g. P. Hoogvliet, *De vita et scriptis Heraclidae Pontici*, Leiden 1858, 100)—whereas the truth is almost the exact opposite (P. Kingsley, *Ancient philosophy, mystery and magic*, Oxford 1995, 292–4). Also worth noting is the fact that according to Heraclides the recognition scene takes place at the temple of Apollo in Didyma, while others prefer various kinds of different settings (including temples of Athena and Hera). It seems not to have been appreciated how appropriate the Didyma location happens to be, not only chronologically (F.A. Carus, *Nachgelassene Werke* iv, Leipzig 1809, 378–9) but also geographically: for Hermotimus the journey down the coast from Clazomenae to Didyma would have been simple and easy. Incidentally, there are writers (e.g. J.D.P. Bolton, *Aristeas of Proconnesus*, Oxford 1962, 200 n.14) who have doubted the existence of any significant connection between Hermotimus and Apollo; but even the details of his murder at the hands of the Cantharidae have a suspiciously close structural similarity to the murder of Orpheus, representative of Apollo, by Dionysian devotees (S. Radt, *Tragicorum Graecorum fragmenta* iii, Göttingen 1985, 138–9; on the Cantharidae cf. e.g. F. Graf, *Nordionische Kulte*, Rome 1985, 390 n.55; and regarding the exclusion of women from Hermotimus' cult, ibid. 392). For the intimate association between Apollo and the practice of lying on the ground, above all in western Asia and those areas closest to Clazomenae both culturally and geographically, see S. Eitrem, *Orakel und Mysterien am Ausgang der Antike* (Zurich 1947) 51–2; P. Kingsley, *In the dark places of wisdom* (Inverness, CA 1999). On the importance of Apollo's role in Clazomenae cf. Graf 384–5; and for the antiquity of his temple at Didyma, as well as its strong ties to Asia, W. Burkert, *The orientalizing revolution* (Cambridge, MA 1992) 60–1 plus his further observations in *Apollo*, ed. J. Solomon (Tucson 1994) 49–60 with note 21 above. And, finally, there is the simple but telling fact that only Heraclides Ponticus' account of the recognition scene happens to obey the strict logic followed by Tibetans as well as Mongols—who are always very specific that what needs to be identified is those possessions belonging to one's immediately preceding incarnation at the time of death.

For Tibetan *tulkus* identifying what belonged to them in their previous incarnation see e.g. A. David-Neel, *With mystics and magicians in Tibet* (London 1931) 124–30; C.A. Bell, *Portrait of a Dalai Lama* (London 1987) 46; The Dalai Lama and G. Rowell, *My Tibet* (Berkeley 1990) 13; D.F. Maher in *The Dalai Lamas*, ed. M. Brauen (Chicago 2005) 132; Chen Qingying, *The system of the Dalai Lama reincarnation* (Beijing 2005) 26; M. Chhaya, *Dalai Lama* (New York 2007) 60–2. But this is not to ignore the fact that in Tibet the procedure was open to blatant manipulation. Cf. S.G. Karmay in *Lhasa in the seventeenth century*, ed. F. Pommaret (Leiden 2003) 68–9 (the case of the Fifth Dalai Lama); and on the increasing abuse of the *tulku* phenomenon in Tibetan Buddhism for political purposes see D. Ermakov's comments, *Bo and Bön* (Kathmandu 2008) 49–50.

The visitors from Hyperborea: cf. J.S. Romm, *The edges of the earth in ancient thought* (Princeton 1992) 61–3 with note 21 above. Of course the narrow-minded view of Athens as the be-all and end-all of the universe was so seductive for many ancient authors including early Platonists (note 19 above), just as it still is for a number of modern writers (e.g. J. Barnes, *International journal of the classical tradition* 4, 1998, 462), that there is a bizarre inevitability about the way some Greeks ended up trying to claim even the Hyperboreans had to be Athenian by origin (S.C. Humphreys, *The strangeness of gods*, Oxford 2004, 103; J. Dillery, *American journal of philology* 126, 2005, 509–10). But if this sounds ridiculous, it really is no more laughable than the childish Athenocentric fantasies we find at the heart of Plato's famous story about Atlantis—where the true heroes and primordial saviors of humanity come neither from Egypt nor, to be sure, from Atlantis but quite miraculously from Athens (*Timaeus* 21e–25c; K.A. Morgan, *Journal of Hellenic studies* 118, 1998, 101–118; S. Broadie, *Oxford studies in ancient philosophy* 21, 2001, 21–8).

"Accompanied by Apollo himself": Herodotus, *Histories* 4.35 (*hama autoisi theoisi apikesthai*), where *theoisi* refers without any doubt to Apollo and his sister.

**24.**

For the early situation in Tibet with regard to Buddhism's simultaneous absorbing of shamanic practices and expelling of its practitioners cf. e.g. W.Y. Evans-Wentz, *The Tibetan book of the great liberation* (Oxford 1954) 26, 179 n.1, 188—who is quite happy to declare Padmasambhava a "Culture Hero" because through his actions "the people of Tibet were elevated from a state of barbarism to a state of unsurpassed spiritual culture"—with the further comments below. For later re-enactments of this same scenario, with oppression and assimilation going hand in hand, see esp. W. Heissig, 'A Mongolian source to the Lamaist suppression of Shamanism in the 17th century,' *Anthropos* 48 (1953) 1–29, 493–536 and *The religions of Mongolia* (London 1980) 36–45 (Mongolia); J.V. Bellezza's overview of the Tibetan picture, *Spirit-mediums, sacred mountains and related Bon textual traditions in Upper Tibet* (Leiden 2005) 10 ("… The cultural history of Tibet over the last millennium would seem to testify to a relentless suppression, assimilation and reconstruction of antecedent legacies in an effort to bring them in compliance with Buddhist sensibilities and tradition …"); and K. Kollmar-Paulenz's comments, on the Fifth Dalai Lama's hostile absorption of other Tibetan Buddhist lineages, in *Biographies of eminent Mongol Buddhists*, ed. J. Elverskog (Halle 2008) 25. That there were very close parallels between Buddhists' treatment of shamanic traditions in Mongolia and in Tibet is beyond any doubt

(Heissig, 'Mongolian source' 24–5; *Religions* 39, 42–3). But apart from such formal analogies, the links between Tibetan and Mongolian shamanism also ran far deeper. As an example of just one particular interaction, note the account in Tibetan records of how at an early date Bön practitioners were banished to "Mongolia and other sparsely populated countries" (Evans-Wentz 188)—a report that gains added interest in light of the fact that this same pattern, of practising shamans being banished by Buddhist lamas to the barren north, would keep repeating itself for a very long time (Heissig, 'Mongolian source' 518). For related evidence of the interweavings between Tibetan Bön and Mongolian shamanism see A. Sárközi in *Synkretismus in den Religionen Zentralasiens*, ed. W. Heissig and H.-J. Klimkeit (Wiesbaden 1987) 120; D. Martin's comments, *Unearthing Bon treasures* (Leiden 2001) 429; J.V. Bellezza, *Zhang Zhung* (Vienna 2008) 557–9; D. Ermakov, *Bo and Bön* (Kathmandu 2008); and for the shamanic aspects of Bön note e.g. S.R. Mumford, *Himalayan dialogue* (Madison, WI 1989) 31 n.3.

On the details, and significance, of the meeting between Sönam Gyatso and Altan Khan see K. Kollmar-Paulenz, *Erdeni tunumal neretü sudur* (Wiesbaden 2001) together with J. Elverskog's commentaries in *The jewel translucent sūtra* (Leiden 2003) 136–81; *Our great Qing* (Honolulu 2006) 101–4; and *Journal of the International Association of Tibetan Studies* 3 (2007) 2–12. The strict formalities of symmetry and reciprocity governing this encounter are not often given the attention they deserve. Historians tend to gravitate towards interpreting what happened exclusively in terms of a traditional Indian relationship between patron and priest (cf. e.g. E. Sperling in *Lhasa in the seventeenth century*, ed. F. Pommaret, Leiden 2003, 121–2). But, first, such relationships in the context of Tibetan Buddhism are far more complex than at first meets the eye (D. Seyfort Ruegg in *Tibetan history and language: Studies dedicated to Uray Géza on his seventieth birthday*, ed. E. Steinkellner, Vienna 1991, 441–53). And second, to view Altan Khan's meeting with the future Dalai Lama only in the light of Indian models is to miss the fact that it also reproduced traditional forms of interaction between earlier Mongol rulers and their shamans: see for example C. Humphrey in *Shamanism, history and the state*, ed. N. Thomas and Humphrey

(Ann Arbor 1996) 202–3 on the exchanging of titles between Genghis Khan and his most famous shaman. This is no more than one among far too many examples of how a purely Tibetocentric (and Buddhocentric) perspective has come to determine historians' understanding of interactions between Mongols and Tibetan Buddhists. On the extremely meaningful process that led early Tibetan Buddhist *tulkus* and missionaries to fill the role of shaman for the Mongols cf. e.g. Heissig, 'Mongolian source' 512–23; C.I. Beckwith, *Journal of the Tibet Society* 7 (1987) 5–11; and see the case of Karma Pakshi discussed below. As for the realities lying behind Altan Khan's conversion to Buddhism, these are also vastly more complex than the fairy-story version that would come to be endorsed by subsequent Dalai Lamas (T. Laird, *The story of Tibet*, New York 2006, 139, 143–5, 420; cf. esp. Elverskog, *Our great Qing* 101–4 with his further comments in *The Mongolia–Tibet interface*, ed. U.E. Bulag and H.G.M. Diemberger, Leiden 2007, 59–80). And as for the title "Dalai Lama" or "Ocean Lama": here, too, the situation is far more subtle and intricate than most Tibetans or westerners are willing to allow. The standard verdict, endorsed by His Holiness the Fourteenth Dalai Lama himself (Laird 142–3), is that it was no more than a clumsy misunderstanding and crude mistranslation by Mongols of Sönam Gyatso's personal name—which quite literally means "ocean of merit." But this is completely to disregard the crucial fact that for Mongols long before the time of Altan Khan (P. Ratchnevsky, *Genghis Khan*, Oxford 1991, 89–90), as well as long after (D. Carruthers, *Unknown Mongolia*, London 1913, 205, 267; W.A. Brown et al., *History of the Mongolian People's Republic*, Cambridge, MA 1976, 782 n.95; Hanzhang Ya, *The biographies of the Dalai Lamas*, Beijing 1991, 41), the name *Dalai* or "Ocean" always had the profoundest importance. Viewed from the Mongol, as opposed to Tibetan, perspective the translation initiated by Altan Khan of the future Dalai Lama's name was an act of creative and transformative significance. For general comments on the related phenomenon of "double etymology," where names and titles are creatively reinterpreted when crossing from one language or culture into another, see P. Kingsley, *Journal of the Warburg and Courtauld Institutes* 56 (1993) 1–24 = *From Poimandres to Jacob Boehme*, ed. R.

van den Broek and C. van Heertum (Amsterdam 2000) 42–76. The now-orthodox attitude of dismissing Altan Khan's initiative, along with its consequences, as misguided and ignorant is just one more symptom of the Tibetocentric attitude that assumes Tibetans must in all matters be intellectually and spiritually superior to the Mongol barbarians.

For a long-overdue challenge to this unquestioned Tibetocentrism see now Elverskog in *The Mongolia–Tibet interface* 59–80, together with Ermakov's gentle but appropriate reminder that "it was the Mongols who initiated the institution of Dalai Lamas" (*Bo and Bön* 660). And as for the title Dalai Lama itself, there is a peculiar irony behind the fact that—whereas His Holiness the Fourteenth Dalai Lama is unwilling to grant it any real significance at all (Laird 143: "'Does the ocean word, *Dalai*, in the Mongolian title, imply something?' ... 'No, there is no implication,' he nearly shouted at me. 'It's just a name!'")—for an understanding of its implications we are obliged to turn to Mongol shamans. See esp. C. Humphrey and U. Onon, *Shamans and elders* (Oxford 1996) 101 ("What does the present mean? It means simply: you have form. But in our mind, having no form is the highest of all. ... And you know that Mongol expression *helber-ugüi Dalai Lam* [literally 'without-shape Ocean Lama']. This means he is above all. And the future is just like the past, going back where you came from. When you die you leave your shape here, you are going to meet your ancestors turning round"); cf. 82.

Finally, a great deal more attention ought to be given to the fact not only that Altan Khan acknowledged the new Dalai Lama as a *tulku* but also that in turn he was recognized by Sönam Gyatso as a *tulku* himself. See e.g. V.L. Uspensky's comments in *Tibet, past and present*, ed. H. Blezer (Leiden 2002) 222–3—and note how consistently the Mongol word *qubilgan* is applied in the *Jewel translucent sūtra* not only to Sönam Gyatso, other Tibetan *tulkus*, and Kublai Khan, but to Altan Khan himself (cf. esp. lines 17, 42, 105, 624–5, 687–8, 812, 844 and 1187 of Elverskog's edition; at 687–8 the formal parallelism between the Dalai Lama as *qubilgan* and Altan Khan as *qubilgan* is unfortunately lost in Elverskog's translation). As soon as one looks beyond the narrowly Tibetan-centered approach to such a crucial encounter between the two men it becomes obvious that for Altan Khan, whose meeting with Sönam Gyatso was in large part inspired by a desperate need to strengthen his very weak link with the ruling lineage of Genghis Khan and Kublai Khan (Elverskog, *Jewel translucent sūtra* 11–15), this recognition was much more necessary than it was for Sönam Gyatso. Very simply, in trying to understand the *tulku* phenomenon of Dalai Lamas from the Tibetan side alone we have been ignoring one half of the equation; and the full significance of all these details will only start to emerge when we see (below) that the famous Tibetan *tulku* tradition was, itself, originally adapted by Buddhist monks for their own religious use from a much older line of rulers. I will just add here, in passing, that only from this perspective are we able to start appreciating what really happened as soon as Sönam Gyatso died. Historians of Tibetan religion are often embarrassed because his reincarnation was discovered in Mongolia, not Tibet. But even more important than the fact that this next Dalai Lama would be a Mongol—or that he would be discovered and formally identified as a reincarnation by the Mongols, on their own, long before any Tibetans became involved (K. Kollmar-Paulenz in *The Dalai Lamas*, ed. M. Brauen, Chicago 2005, 60; M.T. Kapstein, *The Tibetans*, Malden, MA 2006, 134; His Holiness the Fourteenth Dalai Lama's version of what happened, in Laird 147, completely omits the role played by the Mongols)—is the further fact that Sönam Gyatso's successor would be found in the family and bloodline of Altan Khan himself (M. Chhaya, *Dalai Lama*, New York 2007, 23–4). In other words with this first, actual reincarnation of a Dalai Lama the roles of spiritual and worldly ruler would be perfectly united; both Sönam Gyatso and Altan Khan will find their re-embodiment in one and the same human being. And this was not, as historians like to claim, just a matter of political expediency or manipulation. On the contrary: it also shows the remarkable genius of the Mongols in recognizing, and living out, the archetype of the ruler always embedded in the role of *tulku*. Clearly there was a great deal in the ancient shamanic culture of the Mongol people that allowed them to resonate with the *tulku* tradition, and even made them quicker at times to respond to its deepest potential than the Tibetans themselves.

Sönam Gyatso's requirement that Altan Khan exterminate shamanism: cf. e.g. Laird 143; Kollmar-Paulenz, *Erdeni tunumal neretü sudur* 186 §218 = 29r14–15 (*ghani mungqagh böge udaghan-i doroyitaghul-un usadqaju*), 298–9 with nn. 496–8; Elverskog, *Jewel translucent sūtra* 158–9 with n. 287, 270 §884. For the response of Mongols in general see Rintschen's delightful but tragic comments, *Acta ethnographica Academiae Scientiarum Hungaricae* 6 (1958) 441. On the subsequent waves of extermination by Tibetan Buddhists cf. also V. Diószegi, ibid. 10 (1961) 201–2; R. Hutton, *Shamans* (London 2001) 18; O. Purev and G. Purvee, *Mongolian shamanism* (Ulaanbaatar 2004) 53; Ermakov 112–13. And note the beautiful Buddhist *thangka* that portrays Sönam Gyatso serenely watching a Mongol shaman being burned to death: P. Berger and T.T. Bartholomew, *Mongolia* (London 1995) 130–1. The silencing of shamans' songs: Heissig, 'Mongolian source' 515-16. As for the claim, made in a recent study of early Buddhist missionary work among the Mongols which tries a little too hard to soften the sharp edges of the brutal clash between Buddhist monks and Mongol shamans, that "of all the indigenous religious practices and rituals only the worship of the *ongghod*" or ancestral spirits was "challenged and ultimately forbidden" (Kollmar-Paulenz in *Biographies of eminent Mongol Buddhists* 21–2; cf. 23 n.13): apart from the fact that such a general claim is not just misleading but untrue (see e.g. Heissig, 'Mongolian source' 514–18), it also radically underestimates the significance of their *ongghod* for the shamans themselves. To say that "only" this aspect of their lives was forbidden is logically equivalent to telling people they can do anything they choose as long as they live without a heart, or are free to drive a car provided it has no engine.

Naqshbandi Sufis in Lhasa: T. Zarcone, *The Tibet journal* 20/3 (1995) 96–114; and cf. J. Elverskog, *Buddhism and Islam on the Silk Road* (Philadelphia 2010), who also presents an interesting perspective on cross-fertilization of ideas about spiritual rulership between Naqshbandis in Central Asia and Dalai Lamas in Tibet.

For the continuous suppression of Tibetan and Mongolian shamanism on direct orders from the Dalai Lamas themselves see Heissig's comments, *Religions* 36–8. As is well known, the lifetime of the famous Fifth Dalai Lama or "Great Fifth"—under whom the Gelukpa lineage of Tibetan Buddhists became the dominant power in the country—was an especially harsh and brutal period. On the widespread massacres and bloodshed by Gelukpa monks which outsiders only just managed to avert at the very last moment prior to the discovery of the "Great Fifth" cf. S.G. Karmay in *Lhasa in the seventeenth century*, ed. F. Pommaret (Leiden 2003) 67; for the infighting among the Gelukpa themselves see e.g. ibid. 68, 70, 76–7; on the later use by Gelukpa monks of lethal magic against leaders of other Tibetan Buddhist lineages to stop them reaching Beijing so they could talk to the emperor, Elverskog in *The Mongolia–Tibet interface* 66 with n.23 (on the precedent for such actions see his *Our great Qing* 195 n.32); and cf. also I. Baker's comments, *The heart of the world* (New York 2004) 460 n.18. The Great Fifth's own words unambiguously stating his policy against those who stood in his way are not easy to forget: "Make the male lines like trees that have had their roots cut; make the female lines like brooks that have dried up in winter; make the children and grandchildren like eggs smashed against rocks ..." (E. Sperling in *Imagining Tibet: perceptions, projections and fantasies*, ed. T. Dodin and H. Räther, Boston 2001, 318; cf. Elverskog's further comments, *Buddhism and Islam* 221–3). In such circumstances the Tibetan Bön practitioners—who already had been victims of mass murder at the hands of Tibetan Buddhist monks for many centuries, in the name of compassion (R. Vitali, *The kingdoms of Gu.ge Pu.hrang*, Dharamsala 1996, 110, cf. 108)—never really stood a chance. On the crushing of their traditions under the Fifth Dalai Lama, seizure of their lands, forced conversions, see e.g. Karmay 71, 76; Sperling in *Lhasa in the seventeenth century* 124–5. Eventually the Greath Fifth did acknowledge Bön as an independent tradition and reassure its surviving practitioners that they had the right to exist (Karmay 77–80), just as he ended up doing with the other Buddhist traditions he had not completely destroyed (cf. e.g. ibid. 70, 72, 76, on the Karma Kagyus and their Karmapa). But he was a supreme pragmatist; and for him such a formal gesture of acknowledgement was the shrewdest way of pacifying those who had suffered so much while also preventing the remaining embers of resentment from flaring into open mutiny. It will be noted that His Holiness the Fourteenth Dalai Lama renewed his predecessor's official recognition of Bön during the fourth Tulku Conference at Sarnath in 1988. But here, too, political motives were uppermost in His Holiness' mind; and he quite openly explained that he needed the antiquity of Bön to strengthen his position in presenting a unified Tibetan front to the Chinese. For his movement towards restoring the Jonangpa lineage of Tibetan Buddhism, assumed until not long ago to have been wiped out entirely by the Fifth Dalai Lama, on condition that the surviving monks accept a Gelukpa lama as their abbot cf. A. Gruschke's concluding remarks in *Tibet, past and present*, ed. H. Blezer (Leiden 2002) 209; and, regarding the ancient Gelukpa tradition of subsuming all other lineages and teachings to itself, note K.R. Schaeffer's comments in *Power, politics and the reinvention of tradition*, ed. B.J. Cuevas and Schaeffer (Leiden 2006) 194.

On the Tibetan process of rewriting history see G. Schulemann, *Geschichte der Dalai-Lamas* (Wiesbaden 1958) 226; Gruschke 195 n.48; Elverskog, *Jewel translucent sūtra* 143 n.240; Schaeffer 194–5; K. Kollmar-Paulenz in *Images of Tibet in the 19th and 20th centuries*, ed. M. Esposito (Paris 2008) ii 707–24, esp. 720; and cf. also Bellezza, *Zhang Zhung* 202-3. The extent to which this process has now spread to the West is a demonstration of how insidiously it can take on a life all of its own. One of the reasons presented by recent western scholars for refusing to accept the existence of Bön as a Tibetan tradition predating Buddhism is their absurd requirement that, to be accepted as such, it would need to manifest the same highly institutionalized forms we find in Buddhism itself (cf. e.g. B.J. Cuevas, *The hidden history of the Tibetan book of the dead*, New York 2003, 28). As for the other arguments, equally tendentious and methodologically flawed, which have been produced to justify this refusal (so H. Blezer, *Revue d'études tibétaines* 15, November 2008, 421–79): they bear an uncanny resemblance to the arguments once presented with supreme confidence as proving that Orphism was just some literary fantasy instead of a genuine religious phenomenon, until a few graffiti and other pieces of evidence were found that demonstrated with crushing finality how completely a generation of experts had been fooled by its own skepticism (L.

Zhmud, *Hermes* 120, 1992, 159–68; A. Bernabé and A.I. Jiménez San Cristóbal, *Instructions for the netherworld*, Leiden 2008). But these same specialists in Tibetan history also seem quite unaware of how inextricably the new academic fashion for presenting Bön as no more than a form of Buddhist tradition (H. Blezer, *Acta orientalia* 68, 2007, 76; C.I. Beckwith, *Empires of the Silk Road*, Princeton 2009, 414 n.79) is bound up with His Holiness the present Dalai Lama's gracious willingness to acknowledge Bön as a legitimate Buddhist lineage (G. Samuel, *Tantric revisionings*, Farnham 2005, 129)—as well as with the instinctive need of surviving Bön practitioners, much like Mongol shamans, to adapt submissively to the formal standards and intellectual requirements imposed by their Buddhist lords. That need is known as the instinct for survival; and if western scholars end up adding insult to injury by labeling Bön as a "heterodox Buddhist tradition" (C.P. Atwood, *International history review* 26, 2004, 250; Z. Bjerken, *Revue d'études tibétaines* 6, October 2004, 48), this is at least a tolerable price to pay for being allowed to survive. The songs that will take away your heart: Humphrey and Onon 183.

Now we come to the origins of the Tibetan Buddhist *tulku* phenomenon.

Several researchers have strongly suspected, and proposed, that it has close links with non-Buddhist shamanic traditions. See e.g. R.A. Paul in *Spirit possession in the Nepal Himalayas*, ed. J.T. Hitchcock and R.L. Jones (Warminster 1976) 141–51; B.N. Aziz, ibid. 343–60; F. Pommaret, *Les revenants de l'au-delà dans le monde tibétain* (Paris 1989) 156-7; S.B. Ortner, *Ethos* 23 (1995) 355–90. But so far these observations, due mostly to anthropologists working in the field, have been lacking the historical underpinnings they needed. That missing historical documentation is, in fact, easy to provide: it divides into two intimately interrelated areas.

First, there is the basic evidence provided by words and language. The idea of a *tulku* has, quite understandably, come to be associated and then equated with the Buddhist concept of a *nirmāṇakāya* or "emanation body." But what has been overlooked is that this process of selecting a Buddhist correspondence for a Tibetan term is just a secondary phenomenon. Far more crucial is the fact that *tulku*—which also can be spelled out as *sprul sku*—is a fine Tibetan word with a long history, and that we can easily trace it back to its roots in the pre-Buddhist period of the ancient Tibetan kings. In its earliest known form it was applied to the Tibetan rulers themselves and referred to their magical power of transformation: a power that allowed the unalterable quality of dignity and majesty each of them embodied to be reborn with the help of shamanic techniques, time and time again, by being transferred into a younger body whenever needed. Without this constant renewal and reincarnation of their perfectly still, unchanging essence the grass would dry up and everything would go wrong; plagues would break out; the harmony of all existence would be broken and the balance of the elements destroyed; life for nature and people would come to an end. Interestingly, the direct bearing of this ancient royal scenario on what later would become the famous Buddhist *tulku* phenomenon has been noticed by specialists in early Tibetan history—but ignored by students of Tibetan Buddhism as if the whole subject were taboo. See esp. G. Tucci, *The tombs of the Tibetan kings* (Rome 1950) 77–8 n.38, and *East and West* 6 (1955–56) 197–205 (e.g. 200–1: "... *sprul* signifies magic power, the liberty of magic action, magic creation ...") = *Opera minora* (Rome 1971) ii 569–83; H.E. Richardson, *Journal of the Royal Asiatic Society* (1964) 12 ("... points clearly to Bon inspiration") and *A corpus of early Tibetan inscriptions* (London 1985) 39 n.2 ("... magical transformation ..."); N.S. Cutler, *The Tibet journal* 16 / 3 (1991) 42, 46, 51 n.50; Shen-yu Lin, *Revue d'études tibétaines* 12 (March 2007) 109–11. For general clarification of the remarks made by Tucci (*Tombs* 78 n.38; cf. *East and West* 6, 1955–56, 197–202) and Richardson (*Journal of the Royal Asiatic Society* 1964, 12) about Bön as the matrix out of which the Buddhist *tulku* phenomenon would eventually evolve, see S.G. Karmay in *Contributions on Tibetan and Buddhist religion and philosophy*, ed. E. Steinkellner and H. Tauscher (Vienna 1983) 89–103; R.A. Stein, *Bulletin de l'École Française d'Extrême-Orient* 77 (1988) 27–56; Bellezza, *Zhang Zhung*. On the cognate word *'phrul* in ancient Tibetan as specifically meaning magical "incarnation" see e.g. Li Fang-Kuei, *T'oung Pao* 44 (1956) 41 (= K. Iwao et al., *Old Tibetan inscriptions*, Tokyo 2009, 32) and 55 with 57 n.; G. Uray,

*Acta orientalia Academiae Scientiarum Hungaricae* 19 (1966) 252; also L.W.J. van der Kuijp in *Xiyu lishi yuyan yanjiu jikan* iii, ed. Shen Weirong (Beijing 2010) at n.89. On the technicalities of how *sprul* and *'phrul* are interrelated see R.A. Stein, *Bulletin of the School of Oriental and African Studies* 36 (1973) 417, who at the same time (415–22) makes some important comments on the essential power of creative generation and reproduction as well as of illusion and magical transformation implied by both words—which of course explains their use in the context of the ancient kings' numinous ability to reproduce themselves through reincarnation. For some additional remarks on the term *tulku* and its links both with incarnation and with "magically produced illusion or creation," cf. Evans-Wentz 29 n.1; and on the use of the terms *'phrul, sprul,* and *sprul sku* or *tulku* in subsequent Bön tradition, S. Hummel, *Acta orientalia* 36 (1974) 187–8.

So, to state the matter simply, the origins of the Buddhist *tulku* tradition lie in the line of kings stretching back to the heart of ancient Tibet. Buddhist lamas learned how to pick up and renew that broken lineage of kings, adapting the shamanic realities of a royal succession to their altered circumstances as celibate monks and representatives of a new religion. But underlying any formal changes or adaptations was the single thread of magical power always finding a new body for itself so it could stay constantly present in the world as a perpetual source of benefit to every form of life. And there is just a touch of irony to the fact that the author of one detailed study about methods of succession among Tibetans has noted how precisely the Buddhist *tulku* phenomenon emulates the same underlying logic—of "self-generating" successors repeatedly reincarnating a primal spiritual reality—already acted out in the system of the ancient Tibetan kings, although without seeming to be aware of the evidence for just how closely these two systems were connected. See R.A. Paul, *The Tibetan symbolic world* (Chicago 1982) = *The Sherpas of Nepal in the Tibetan cultural context* (Delhi 1989) 38–41.

Regarding the second direction we need to look towards for an understanding of the *tulku* phenomenon: this of course is its point of origin inside Buddhism itself. And one particular person stands at that originating point—somebody called Karma Pakshi. He was born early in the 13th century at the eastern edge of Tibet, and became a remarkably open-minded Buddhist in his life as well as his writings. This open-mindedness was one of the factors that drew him to spend much of his later life among the Mongols, giving him an exposure to Mongolian practices and traditions whose importance for understanding Karma Pakshi's achievements should not be underestimated. He saw it as a significant part of his work to help support other, non-Buddhist religions and he felt a special sympathy for the religious tolerance of the Khans who honored ancient shamanic principles in allowing people under their rule the freedom to follow their own tradition (cf. esp. M.T. Kapstein, *The Tibetan assimilation of Buddhism*, New York 2000, 97–106, 244 n.81, with note 29 below; for Karma Pakshi on the Silk Road, in the region of the Tarim Basin, around the Gobi Desert and elsewhere see L. Terhune's comments, *Karmapa*, Boston 2004, 78 with van der Kuijp in *Xiyu lishi yuyan yanjiu jikan*). And it was by Mongols, at the courts of the Khans, that he was given the name Pakshi or Bagshi: the Mongolian name traditionally reserved for shamans (N. Prejevalsky, *Mongolia, the Tangut country and the solitudes of northern Tibet* i, London 1876, xxxiv–xxxv; Diószegi, *Acta ethnographica Academiae Scientiarum Hungaricae* 10, 1961, 201; Beckwith, *Journal of the Tibet Society* 7, 1987, 6–8; Humphrey in *Shamanism, history and the state* 202, 206 n.17; and cf. also L.W.J. van der Kuijp, *Central Asiatic Journal* 39, 1995, 275–302 for the word's introduction into the Tibetan language; T. Gibson, *Numen* 44, 1997, 50–1, gets the history of the word's connection with Buddhism back to front). He was well known for his powers of ecstasy (G.N. Roerich, *The blue annals*, Calcutta 1949, 487; M. Rossabi, *Khubilai Khan*, Berkeley 1988, 40), notorious for his sorcery (H.E. Richardson, *Journal of the Royal Asiatic Society* 1958, 142–5), and became especially famous for his healing abilities as well as for balancing and bringing back into harmony all the elements of nature wherever he went (N. Douglas and M. White, *Karmapa*, London 1976, 43; Karma Thinley, *The history of the sixteen Karmapas of Tibet*, Boulder 1980, 48–9; R. Dunnell, *Asia Major* 5/1, 1992, 102). But one of his most important achievements was to initiate the

Tibetan Buddhist system of *tulku* reincarnations. Naturally there had been Indian and Tibetan teachers long before him who were sometimes considered reincarnations of earlier figures (cf. e.g. L.W.J. van der Kuijp in *The Dalai Lamas*, ed. M. Brauen, Chicago 2005, 28–9 and, for a significant Chinese background to the Karma Kagyu lineage, E. Sperling in *Journal of the Tibet Society* 7, 1987, 37–9). That was nothing new; but it was Karma Pakshi who specifically would be given credit for creating the Buddhist *tulku* institution as a conscious, self-contained system of rebirth with its set formalities and procedures (Thinley 22; G. Samuel, *Civilized shamans*, Washington, DC 1993, 494; Kapstein, *Tibetan assimilation* 99; Terhune, *Karmapa* 282 n.39; van der Kuijp in *The Dalai Lamas* 28; Chen Qingying, *The system of the Dalai Lama reincarnation*, Beijing 2005, 6–7). And, when we look a little closer, we can see he was given the credit for this with very good reason. The transfer of authority from his Karmapa predecessor, Düsum Khyenpa, to him had been a convoluted and long-drawn-out affair (Roerich 482–5). But even more significantly, the initial efforts that Karma Pakshi himself would put into arranging his own reincarnation just before he died turned out to be appalling failures. His first attempt, at transferring his consciousness directly into a child, was a disaster (cf. the account in Roerich 487–8 and, for the Indian origins of this technique, M. Nihom in *Ritual, state and history in South Asia*, ed. A.W. van den Hoek et al., Leiden 1992, 239 n.42). His second attempt, by inserting his consciousness into a woman's womb, would be more successful but also would create a huge amount of confusion and uncertainty among his disciples (Roerich 488; Kapstein, *Tibetan assimilation* 243 n.56; this is a technique well known to shamans: cf. e.g. M. Eliade, *Shamanism*, Princeton 1962, 246). Clearly everything was still being discovered, step by step, with Karma Pakshi using all his experience and resourcefulness to bring the pieces together from wherever he could find them until he created a recognizable system that worked.

But this leaves open the question of why Karma Pakshi of all people, rather than anybody else either after or before him, happened to be the particular Buddhist who ended up bringing such a famous institution into being. The question is a crucial one but, as often is the case with crucial questions, is so important it never gets asked; and the answer happens to be staring us so directly in the face that there is something incredible about the way no one would seem even to have noticed it. This is the fact, emphasized by ancient biographers, that Karma Pakshi was an exceptional Buddhist in his time because he was descended from a royal bloodline and had been born into a family which traced its origins back to the old Tibetan kings (Roerich 485; Thinley 47; Richardson, *Journal of the Royal Asiatic Society* 1958, 141). His direct link to the ancient lineage of royal incarnations—powered and kept alive by the magical potency of *sprul* or *'phrul* which, even on the most basic linguistic level, relates straight to the word *tulku* itself—could hardly be plainer. I should record that when I first came across this evidence, and realized the importance of Karma Pakshi's royal origins, what bewildered me most was the complete and total silence about it on the part of western as well as Tibetan scholars. But one day I was delighted to receive from Daniel Berounský in Prague the unpublished draft of a paper he has written, called 'Entering dead bodies and the miraculous power of the kings: notes on Karma Pakshi's reincarnation in Tibet.' It was a real joy, not to mention an enormous relief, to find that at last I was no longer alone in noticing these crucial details and seeing their significance.

I do need to add one final point, however—which takes us the next step beyond even such an important issue as Karma Pakshi's royal descent. This is that, in reviving the centuries-old lineage of royal incarnations, he was motivated by far more than just some nostalgic or sentimental reminiscence for the days of the ancient empire. Karma Pakshi was not a dreamer but, as even his name indicates, a man of action; and there are two separate factors that show just how much more was at stake than vague romanticism. First, evidence exists that indicates he himself put a great deal of effort into not only concretizing but also activating a connection between his Karma Kagyu lineage of Tibetan Buddhism—the line he himself was the head of—and the lineage of old Tibetan kings. During the 1940s the British diplomat Hugh Richardson came across a stone pillar, inscribed with an ancient royal text from the time of the Dharma King Ralpacan, in the courtyard of the main Karma Kagyu monastery to the west of Lhasa. The monks themselves could hardly have shown less curiosity about the pillar, as is so often the case in such situations; but when all the various facts are considered and pieced together, everything points to the conclusion that Karma Pakshi himself went to the enormous trouble of having it brought to his monastery and relocated there. See Richardson's descriptions and comments, *Journal of the Royal Asiatic Society* (1958) 139–41; for another example of Karma Pakshi going to enormous lengths to have a huge object transported to this same monastery at Tsurphu, compare Douglas and White 44; and for the formulaic term *'phrul* as applied specifically to Ralpacan cf. P.K. Sørensen, *The mirror illuminating the royal genealogies* (Wiesbaden 1994) 416, 417 n.1456, with Richardson, *Journal of the Royal Asiatic Society of Bengal* 15 (1949) 62 n.2. One thing we can say with absolute certainty is that Karma Pakshi was not the kind of person to get involved in having pillars moved around Tibet on a whim or without a very deep purpose. His link to Tibetan royalty was plainly a great deal more than just a memory. This is something he was determined to manifest, to demonstrate in the physical world using every symbolic means possible, so he could transfer the realities of the past into the present and make them real again.

And there is one other reason why we can be sure Karma Pakshi's motivations were much more than just sentimental or romantic. His and his successors' attempts to revive the ancient line of Tibetan kings for their Karma Kagyu lineage may have ended in failure: the time would eventually come when they were smacked down and decisively squashed by the Gelukpa lineage of the Dalai Lamas. But ironically it was the "Great Fifth," the Fifth Dalai Lama himself, who by dominating the whole of Tibet was at last able to succeed where Karma Pakshi had tried and failed. Very consciously, and with the greatest attention to detail, the Great Fifth presented himself as the ruler who had managed to revive the ancient line of Tibetan kings and bring their heritage back to life (D.S. Lopez in *New Qing imperial history*, ed. J.A. Millward et al., London 2004, 26–7; K. Kollmar-Paulenz, *Kleine Geschichte Tibets*, Munich 2006, 113; J. Powers, *Introduction to Tibetan Buddhism*, 2nd ed., Ithaca, NY 2007, 165-6, 168). This revival was a wonderful rallying cry for the Dalai Lamas; but to see it as just the result of some arbitrary, political drive for power would be to miss what is most essential. It happened because, with the Great Fifth and all subsequent Dalai Lamas down to the Fourteenth, the institution of the Buddhist *tulku* had at last ended up becoming exactly what its pre-Buddhist genes always urged it to be—constant rebirth for the magical ruler, with his ancient shamanic powers, over the whole of Tibet.

## 25.

For reincarnation, and identification of one's belongings from the previous lifetime, in British Columbia see especially Antonia Mills in *Amerindian rebirth*, ed. Mills and R. Slobodin (Toronto 1994) 213; also her touching contemporary descriptions and comments in *Anthropologica* 30 (1988) 30, 37-8, 43. It will be noted that this process of identifying belongings from the previous lifetime typically used to focus on the figures of tribal leaders (Mills in *Amerindian rebirth* 213; for reincarnation of tribal chiefs cf. also Mills, *Canadian journal of native studies* 21, 2001, 312-15)—which agrees perfectly with what we have already seen about the early Tibetan history of the *tulku* institution (above, note 24). On the broad spread of reincarnation beliefs and practices among American Indians see Mills' summary, *Journal of anthropological research* 44 (1988) 385-6, together with the various contributions to *Amerindian rebirth*.

For general comments on the immense significance and antiquity of the great migrations via land and sea from eastern Asia to the Americas by people, notably ancestors of present-day Mongols, who would become the tribes now known as indigenous American Indians see e.g. S.E. Hollimon in *The archaeology of shamanism*, ed. N.S. Price (London 2001) 123-5; P.N. Jones, *Respect for the ancestors* (Boulder 2005); C.C. Mann, *1491* (New York 2006); D. Ermakov, *Bo and Bön* (Kathmandu 2008) 1-2, 59-60, 393 n.14; D.J. Meltzer, *First peoples in a new world* (Berkeley 2009); and below, note 30. On the genetic evidence for these migrations, especially from the region of Mongolia, cf. C.J. Kolman et al., *Genetics* 142 (1996)

1321–34; D.A. Merriwether et al., *American journal of human genetics* 59 (1996) 204–12 and M.C. Dulik et al., ibid. 90 (2012) 1–18; S.L. Bonatto and F.M. Salzano, *Proceedings of the National Academy of Sciences of the United States of America* 94 (1997) 1866–71; Jones 97–105, 112, 192; A. Kitchen et al., *PLoS One* 3/2 (2008) e1596; M. Rasmussen et al., *Nature* 506 (2014) 225–9. For the linguistic evidence see M. Swadesh, *American anthropologist* 64 (1962) 1262–91; M. Fortescue, *Language relations across Bering Strait* (London 1998); A. Berge in *Concise encyclopedia of languages of the world*, ed. K. Brown and S. Ogilvie (Oxford 2009) 371; C. Holden, *Science* 319 (03.21.2008) 1595 with E. Vajda, *Anthropological papers of the University of Alaska* 5 (2010) 35–120. The comparative evidence based on astronomical and mythological traditions is also extremely significant: W.B. Gibbon, *Journal of American folklore* 77/305 (1964) 236–50 and 85/337 (1972) 236–47; J.A. Stewart in *The 8th international congress of Mongolists being convened under the patronage of N. Bagabandi* (Ulaanbaatar 2002) 173–4; Y. Berezkin, *Folklore* 31 (2005) 79–100. And it will be noted not only that there are Native American traditions compatible with the realities of a trans-Pacific crossing but that some indigenous people quite explicitly interpret their own legends in this way (A.F.C. Wallace and W.D. Reyburn, *International journal of American linguistics* 17, 1951, 42–7; Chien Chiao, *Continuation of tradition in Navajo society*, Taipei 1971; J. Paper, *A material case for a late Bering Strait crossing coincident with pre-Columbian trans-Pacific crossings*, Philadelphia 1993, 4–5; J.A.P. Wilson, *Limina* 11, 2005, 68–9).

I. Stevenson (*Twenty cases suggestive of reincarnation*, 2nd ed., Charlottesville 1974, 217–19; cf. also J.A.P. Wilson, *Critique of anthropology* 28, 2008, 267–78) tried to explain the spread of ideas and practices relating to reincarnation from east Central Asia to the American continent as due to contact between Asian Buddhists and American Indians; but Mills has correctly emphasized that such recent contact could in no way come even close to accounting for the dispersion, as well as the nature, of these ideas and practices throughout North America (*Anthropologica* 30, 1988, 45–6; *Amerindian rebirth* 19–20). For reincarnation in the context of pre-Buddhist Mongolian and Siberian shamanism see Ermakov 523, 558–9, and cf. also W. Ruben, *Acta orientalia* 18 (1940) 187; E.R.

Dodds, *The Greeks and the irrational* (Berkeley 1956) 165 n.56; Mills in *Amerindian rebirth* 36 n.4; R. Slobodin, ibid. 137; J.P. Berkey, *The formation of Islam* (Cambridge 2003) 246. This shamanic dimension of beliefs and practices related to rebirth is inseparably bound up with the enormous importance attributed by shamans to inheriting the spirits of ancestors (for which see W. Heissig, *Anthropos* 48, 1953, 508–10; L. Krader, *Southwestern journal of anthropology* 10, 1954, 333-4; Dodds 144; W. Burkert, *Lore and science in ancient Pythagoreanism*, Cambridge, MA 1972, 163; G. Obeyesekere in *Amerindian rebirth* xiv) as well as animals (C. Humphrey and U. Onon, *Shamans and elders*, Oxford 1996, 99–105). On the intimate links between reincarnation and shamanism in general cf. e.g. P. Radin, *Primitive religion* (New York 1937) 270–5 and in *Amerindian rebirth* 55-66; Mills, *Anthropologica* 30 (1988) 45–6, *Amerindian rebirth* 4, 8, 18 and *Canadian journal of native studies* 21 (2001) 311–12; and the poignant first-hand comments by C. Matchatis, *Shaman* 13 (2005) 104-5 with n.4. Those western historians (e.g. C.H. Kahn in *Essays in ancient Greek philosophy*, ed. J.P. Anton and G.L. Kustas, Albany 1971, 32-5; T. McEvilley, *The shape of ancient thought*, New York 2002, 120) who deny the existence of any such connection between shamanism and rebirth show not only a remarkable degree of unfamiliarity with the factors involved but also an equally remarkable adherence to the old, self-reinforcing myths about "higher" and "lower" cultures. Reincarnation in Hinduism and Buddhism is of course not an early phenomenon (W. Halbfass, *Tradition and reflection*, Albany, NY 1991, 291–2)—and to assume the influence here of shamanism on the great Indian religions, just as on Greek religion, is a very logical conclusion (cf. e.g. C. von Fürer-Haimendorf, *Journal of the Royal Anthropological Institute of Great Britain and Ireland* 83, 1952, 37–49; Dodds 172 n.97; Mills, *Anthropologica* 30, 1988, 45; also G. Obeyesekere's comments, *Imagining karma*, Berkeley 2002, 89). Regarding the transfer of specifically Central Asian shamanic traditions down into India see J.E. Mitchiner, *Traditions of the seven Ṛṣis* (Delhi 1982), esp. 188–9; E.C.L. During Caspers in *Ritual, state and history in South Asia*, ed. A.W. van den Hoek et al. (Leiden 1992) 102–27 and in *South Asian archaeology 1991*, ed. A.J. Gail et al. (Stuttgart 1993) 65–86; P.

145

Gignoux, *Man and cosmos in ancient Iran* (Rome 2001) 74–5, 86–91; the unfortunate but predictable insistence of many Indologists on over-rationalizing their chosen area of study (cf. e.g. A. Sumegi, *Dreamworlds of shamanism and Tibetan Buddhism*, Albany 2008, 135 n.64) sadly tends to obscure the evidence for such transfers and transitions, just as happens with the study of the Greeks (see my comments in *Studia Iranica* 23, 1994, 187–98).

Gananath Obeyesekere follows another line of rationalizing when he insists on "manipulating" the evidence, in line with Weber's theories, so as to produce a fundamental contrast between the "ethicized" reincarnation beliefs of Hindus or Buddhists and the "unethicized" reincarnation beliefs of indigenous peoples (*Imagining karma*, and in *Amerindian rebirth* xix–xxiii). But as Mills points out (ibid. 16–18), this is nothing but a caricature of the traditions as preserved and lived by indigenous people—who have their own very highly developed systems of ethics. And one should add a question as to what is really more ethical: to be obsessed with one's own individual salvation as in the "higher" religions of India, or to be constantly engaged with practising respect and consideration towards all forms of life in an overall framework of concern for the welfare of both visible and invisible worlds. See also S. F. Teiser in *Journal of ritual studies* 19 (2005) 147–52 for other criticisms of Obeyesekere's theories about "ethicization" (which Obeyesekere in his retort, ibid. 160–4, does nothing to answer). I should perhaps add that unfortunately Obeyesekere makes an utter mess of the Greek material (e.g. *Imagining karma* 201–4) and, although he likes sometimes to misquote me so as to give support to his strange theories, has no understanding in particular of the role reserved for Apollo by the Greeks (on which see Kingsley, *In the dark places of wisdom*, Inverness, CA 1999, and note 21 above). As for the idea—closely related to the concept of "ethicization," and so common among Buddhists as well as westerners—that shamanic traditions have no access to the "transcendent," this is another myth which Mills (*Amerindian rebirth* 17–18) helps in a wise and timely fashion to put to rest. The fact that a transcendent realm beyond the senses happens, in the hands of most true elders and shamans, to be seamlessly interwoven with this world to the point where the two become one is a sign not of inferiority but of a far greater capacity for integration.

Finally, it should be noted that this overall scenario—of reincarnation beliefs and practices being disseminated from eastern Central Asia not only further eastwards into North America but also westwards, as with Abaris, into the world of the ancient Greeks—provides the perfect basis for understanding how the famous complex of Orpheus traditions appears not just in the Greek world but also among the native people of North America. See Å. Hultkrantz's remarkable study, *The North American Indian Orpheus tradition* (Stockholm 1957), esp. 183–210; and cf. F. Graf's comments in *Interpretations of Greek mythology*, ed. J.N. Bremmer (London 1987) 83–4. On the background of Asiatic shamanic traditions behind the Orpheus myths see e.g. K. Meuli, *Gesammelte Schriften* (Basel 1975) ii 697, 871–3, 1031; Hultkrantz 191–2, 198–9, 236–63; M.L. West, *The Orphic poems* (Oxford 1983) 3–7 with n.8; C. Ginzburg, *Ecstasies* (New York 1991) 254 with n.187; F. Thordarson in *The Nart epic and Caucasology*, ed. A.M. Gadagatl' and R.G. Khadzhebiekov (Maykop 1994) 347–8; P. Kingsley, *Ancient philosophy, mystery and magic* (Oxford 1995) 226; A.-L. Siikala in Siikala and M. Hoppál, *Studies on shamanism* (2nd ed., Budapest 1998) 85; Gignoux 83; P. De Luca, *Il logos sensibile di María Zambrano* (Soveria Mannelli 2004) 45 n.17.

## 26.

For complaints about the supposed impossibility of Greeks traveling into Central Asia see e.g. S. West in *Pontus and the outside world*, ed. C.J. Tuplin (Leiden 2004) 54–60 ("immense practical difficulties … a hard journey … linguistic problems … intellectual barriers … extremely demanding"). There is a very predictable inevitability in the way that, when distinguishing impossibilities from possibilities, historians tend to side with the lazy and appeal to the lowest common denominator—not even noticing that according to their own criteria the best-attested cases of physical exploration, or intimate participation in the spiritual worlds of other cultures, would be completely unimaginable. As for the fact that people, religious traditions, technical know-how had already been crisscrossing the entire length and breadth of Asia well before the time of Abaris or Pythagoras (cf. e.g. V.H. Mair, *Early China* 15, 1990, 27–47 and *The shorter Columbia anthology of traditional Chinese literature*, New York 2000, 194n., with note 27 below): this is evidently a mere nuisance best handled by being ignored. And the same basic story repeats itself when classical scholars insist on emphasizing how utterly alarmed "the Greeks" were at even the prospect of venturing out by sea beyond the familiarity of the Mediterranean, or how certain philosophers such as Plato considered it a virtue to avoid any unsupervised contact with foreign people and cultures (see e.g. Pindar, *Olympian odes* 3.43–5; Plato, *Laws* 949e–953e with B.H. Isaac, *The invention of racism in classical antiquity*, Princeton 2004, 239–42). But almost nothing is said about those Greeks who century after century were quietly making a mockery of every racial stereotype by sailing far out into the Atlantic and down the coast of Africa or up to the Arctic Circle, mapping the earth, discovering it was a sphere, providing the material that Plato would use for some of his most outlandish myths—only to be accused by other Greeks and then Romans of inventing ridiculous children's stories or being the most outrageous of liars (P. Kingsley, *Reality*, Inverness, CA 2003).

In the case of Central Asia, another assumption automatically comes into play: that no Greeks in their right minds would even have dreamed of venturing into such a barren area, devoid of any civilized traces. But some students of world history are at last coming back to the realization already articulated by great explorers of the nineteenth century, which is that Central Asia used to be far more than just some gaping hole separating the supposedly "high" cultures of the Mediterranean and Near East from India and China. In fact it has always been a region of immensely sophisticated complexity, a little of which can be appreciated by European eyes but much of which never can be, culture upon culture. See e.g. F. von Richthofen, *The geographical magazine* 1 (July 1874) 144–6; W.B. Lincoln, *The conquest of a continent* (New York 1994) 49–50; V. Elisseeff, *The Silk Roads* (Oxford 2000) 2; N. Di Cosmo, *Ancient*

*China and its enemies* (Cambridge 2002); C. Beckwith, *Empires of the Silk Road* (Princeton 2009).

The notorious issue about "the Greeks" not being able to understand foreign languages is one of the most embarrassing follies of modern scholarship. The insane idea that Greeks as a whole had neither the ability nor the will to learn foreign languages has been popularized by academics who should have known far better. Cf. e.g. Arnaldo Momigliano's classic announcement that "Greek remained the only language of civilization for every Greek-speaking man … the Greeks were seldom in a position to check what the natives told them: they did not know the languages" (*Alien wisdom*, Cambridge 1975, 8, cf. 148–9), and the outpouring of complaints in philosophy manuals about "the linguistic obstacles to intellectual communication between Greeks and orientals" (J. Brunschwig in *The Cambridge history of Hellenistic philosophy*, ed. K. Algra et al., Cambridge 1999, 241). But these sweeping generalizations say more about the outright bias, and naïveté, of scholars in the modern western world than about ancient Greece. To talk about "the Greeks" is as ridiculous as talking about "the Europeans" or "the Americans." It goes without saying that most people had then, just as they have now, no wish or need to learn a foreign language; but in the case of traders, traveling craftsmen, adventurers, explorers, diplomats, mercenaries and many other kinds of professionals or specialists or curious individuals, not to mention people already brought up and living on the very edges of the Greek-speaking world, the situation happened to be totally different. Foreign words and languages were always learned by travelers when needed, without any dictionaries or formal schooling; and the constant movements of people together with ancient trade networks (note 27 below) will have meant that the phenomenon of interpreters able to mediate between the Greek language and the languages of Central Asia, in particular, was far more common than we are willing to suppose. Cf. e.g. A.M. Frenkian, *L'Orient et les origines de l'idéalisme subjectif dans la pensée européenne* i (Paris 1946) 29–30; D.J. Mosley, *Ancient society* 2 (1971) 1–6; D. Asheri, *Fra ellenismo e iranismo* (Bologna 1983) 16–25; P.

Briant, *L'Asie centrale et les royaumes proche-orientaux du premier millénaire* (Paris 1984) 94–6; S. Sherwin-White in *Hellenism in the East*, ed. A. Kuhrt and Sherwin-White (London 1987) 1–31; P. Kingsley, *Studia Iranica* 23 (1994) 195–6; F. Thordarson, *Symbolae Osloenses* 71 (1996) 54–5; M.L. West, *The east face of Helicon* (Oxford 1997); T. McEvilley, *The shape of ancient thought* (New York 2002) 1–13; L. Gemelli Marciano, *Die Vorsokratiker* i (Düsseldorf 2007) 405–6; A. Kuhrt, *The Persian Empire* (Abingdon 2007) ii 842–8. And any idea that the ancient world had to wait for Alexander the Great to stir the pot by precipitating an interpenetrating of different cultures or languages would be a major misconception. Alexander was simply working with the tendencies already activated and in full force long before his time (P. Kingsley, *Journal of the Royal Asiatic Society* 5, 1995, 188–9, 198–206; S. Dalley and A.T. Reyes in *The legacy of Mesopotamia*, ed. Dalley, Oxford 1998, 111). In the case of Pythagoras, who became notorious because of his extensive journeys into strange countries (note 20 above; below, note 27), the fact that his own father happened to be a craftsman whose work involved large amounts of travel and communication with non-Greeks is certainly no coincidence (P. Kingsley, *Journal of the Warburg and Courtauld Institutes* 57, 1994, 2). As for Aristeas of Proconnesus (notes 2 and 15 above), it helps to remember that he came from what now is a Turkish island on the edge of Asia—in other words from a border region famous for producing bilingual or trilingual speakers and interpreters (M.C. Miller, *Athens and Persia in the fifth century BC*, Cambridge 2004, 132). This is not even to mention the fact that his father's name clearly reveals the family's non-Greek origin (for the name Kaystrobios mentioned in Herodotus' *Histories* 4.13 cf. O. Szemerényi's comments, *Journal of Hellenic studies* 94, 1974, 155).

A major trend in recent scholarship is to dismiss the realities of contact between ancient Greeks and foreigners as too "complex" for study, or even as "a distraction," and to focus instead on analyzing the illusory fantasies about different cultures which we are asked to believe Greeks in their isolated ignorance loved to spend their time spinning: see e.g. T. Harrison's programmatic statements in *Greeks and barbarians* (Edinburgh 2001) 9–14. That could sound bizarre, because before understanding the illusions one naturally has to know the realities; but such a back-to-front procedure is very much in line with modern preferences for focusing on fantasy instead of reality. The simple truth is that, until classicists start noticing the evidence in front of their own eyes, they really have no right whatsoever to talk about insuperable language barriers in the ancient world—or even to go to the extent of depicting Greeks as people who were "fed on forgeries" because they had virtually no access to genuine sources of knowledge about oriental traditions, even less interest in finding those sources or using them, and agreed to be nourished on cheap substitutes instead (Momigliano 148).

For instance Momigliano (141–8) explicitly includes Plato along with Plato's immediate circle in his influential portrayal of Greek intellectuals being nourished on forgeries, instead of authentic sources, about the traditions of other cultures. But this is only because he has no knowledge at all about the almost endless examples of perfectly genuine oriental expressions and religious, cosmological or astronomical traditions of specifically oriental origin embedded in the writings of Plato as well as Plato's circle: examples that have been overlooked, misunderstood, mistranslated and even edited out of the original Greek texts by generation after generation of scholars so untouched by oriental cultures they have absolutely no way of recognizing what they are confronted with. See e.g. P. Kingsley, *Journal of the Royal Asiatic Society* 5 (1995) 201–7 with A.D.H. Bivar, *The personalities of Mithra in archaeology and literature* (New York 1998) 78 and W. Burkert, *Babylon, Memphis, Persepolis* (Cambridge, MA 2004) 68. If one were painstakingly to document and bring together each item of evidence demonstrating the oriental source and inspiration for Plato's ideas—from the famous myth at the end of the *Phaedo*, from the even more famous myth of Er, not to mention many other places—this would force a dramatic reassessment of his philosophy as a whole. But in the larger scheme of things that would make no difference at all. The vessel of the western intellect is cracked beyond repair, completely unable any longer to contain the fullness of life; and Plato himself, through his rationalizing of older traditions, is to a considerable extent responsible for that fracturing. Cf. P. Kingsley, *Ancient philosophy, mystery and magic* (Oxford 1995), esp. 158; *Reality* 126–8, 303–6.

## 27.

Europeans in the Tarim Basin: E.W. Barber, *The mummies of Ürümchi* (New York 1999); J.P. Mallory and V.H. Mair, *The Tarim mummies* (London 2000); V.H. Mair in *Proceedings of the sixteenth annual UCLA Indo-European conference*, ed. K. Jones-Bley et al. (Washington, DC 2005) 1–46; D. Ermakov, *Bo and Bön* (Kathmandu 2008) 712–14; E.E. Kuzmina, *The prehistory of the Silk Road* (Philadelphia 2008) 88–98; J. Romgard, *Questions of ancient human settlements in Xinjiang and the early Silk Road trade, with an overview of the Silk Road research institutions and scholars in Beijing, Gansu, and Xinjiang* (Sino-Platonic papers 185, Philadelphia 2008). As noted by Kuzmina (91–2), it was these migrations from Europe to Xinjiang that essentially laid much of the ground for what a great deal later would become the "Silk Road." This vast complex of ancient evidence naturally makes a complete mockery of western historians' fears about allowing Aristeas, in particular, to penetrate far into Asia at an early date: note already, on this matter, A. Alemany i Vilamajó's sensible comments, *Faventia* 21/2 (1999) 47 n.3, with Mallory and Mair 39–45. For some very apt general observations on the interconnectedness of East and West in the ancient world, and its relevance to us today, see Romgard 5–6. And on the arrival of items from China in Europe, including classical Greece, centuries before what western historians traditionally consider the official opening of the Silk Road see H.-J. Hundt, *Jahrbuch des Römisch-Germanischen Zentralmuseums Mainz* 16 (1969) 59–71; J. Needham and D. Kühn, *Science and civilisation in China* v/9 (Cambridge 1988) 418; V.H. Mair, *Early China* 15 (1990) 44; M.C. Miller, *Athens and Persia in the fifth century BC* (Cambridge 2004) 77–81; Kuzmina 1–7; Romgard 9, 24; and cf. also J. Wiesner, *Jahrbuch des Deutschen Archäologischen Instituts* 78 (1963) 212.

For the antiquity, and authenticity, of traditions about Pythagoras' distant journeys see P. Kingsley, *Journal of the Warburg* and Courtauld Institutes 57 (1994) 1–13; In the dark places of wisdom (Inverness, CA 1999) 12–18, 237–8; Lapis 10 (1999) 63–8; above, note 26. Documentation provided by studies such as H. Luschey's (Archaeologische Mitteilungen aus Iran 1, 1968, 88–9), U. Jantzen's (Ägyptische und orientalische Bronzen aus dem Heraion von Samos, Bonn 1972), H. Kyrieleis' (Jahrbuch des Deutschen Archäologischen Instituts 94, 1979, 32–48 and in Greek sanctuaries, ed. N. Marinatos and R. Hägg, London 1993, 145–9), O.W. Muscarella's (The catalogue of ivories from Hasanlu, Iran, Philadelphia 1980), S. Dalley's (The legacy of Mesopotamia, Oxford 1998, 98, 104, 107) and F. Sciacca's (Patere baccellate in bronzo, Rome 2005) should be more than enough to show how very wide the door happened to stand open between various parts of Asia and Pythagoras' home island of Samos in particular. And for the specific bearing of Pythagoras' own unique links with Hyperborea (above, note 21) on the many traditions about his foreign travels see K. Karttunen's appropriate comments, India in early Greek literature (Helsinki 1989) 115.

In this context the striking report about Pythagoras being well known, after he had returned from his travels, for wearing trousers (Aelian, Historical miscellany 12.32) is certainly significant. Wearing trousers was almost a taboo in Athens and elsewhere: they were far "too foreign" for a respectable Greek to be seen in (Miller 184–6; H. Tell, Classical antiquity 26, 2007, 255, shows no awareness of the factors involved). In connection with Pythagoras, they are usually described as "a sure pointer toward the Iranian–Scythian area" (W. Burkert, Lore and science in ancient Pythagoreanism, Cambridge, MA 1972, 165; "Persian or Scythian": ibid. 112 n.16); and no less sure is the fact that Samos had the closest of ties, both commercial and diplomatic, with Iran (P. Kingsley, Studia Iranica 23, 1994, 192 n.21). But as far as the trousers are concerned, we can be a little more specific. Trousers were worn for convenience and warmth throughout the steppe regions of northern Iran and Central Asia by horse-riding nomads, not only men but also women, back in time as far as we can see (D. Christian, A history of Russia, Central Asia and Mongolia i, Oxford 1998, 163; Barber 25, 37–9, 188; Mallory and Mair 8, 41, 79, 138, 155, 212–22; J. Davis-Kimball, Warrior women, New York 2002, 99–101; Mair, Contact and exchange in the ancient *world*, Honolulu 2006, 1). On the other hand early Persians, even when riding to war, are shown wearing not trousers but tunics (see esp. the evidence discussed in D.T. Potts, *The archaeology of Elam*, Cambridge 1999, 340–1); and the adoption of trousers by Persians can only be confirmed for a period after the time of Pythagoras (A.S. Shahbazi, *Encyclopaedia Iranica* v / 7, Costa Mesa 1992, 733–5). While on the subject of Central Asian nomads it should be noted as well, in passing, that the white-colored clothing and golden crown also associated with Pythagoras (Aelian, loc. cit.) would remain standard shamanic regalia across Central Asia not only for hundreds but for thousands of years: cf. e.g. W. Heissig, *The religions of Mongolia* (London 1980) 6 and P. Ratchnevsky, *Genghis Khan* (Oxford 1991) 101 with T.T. Allsen, *Commodity and exchange in the Mongol empire* (Cambridge 1997) 57–60; K. Pratt and R. Rutt, *Korea* (Richmond, Surrey 1999) 145, 413, 473–5 with their further references. For the significant stories that unfamiliar items of clothing are easily capable of telling see P. Kingsley, *Ancient philosophy, mystery and magic* (Oxford 1995) 233–316; J. Bollansée in *Die Fragmente der griechischen Historiker* IVA / 3 (Leiden 1999) 455 with n.25; D.F. Launderville, *Spirit and reason* (Waco 2007) 319.

Then there is Pythagoras' custom of speaking from behind a curtain (Iamblichus, *Pythagorean life* 72 and 89; cf. Diogenes Laertius, *Lives and views of famous philosophers* 8.10 with Burkert 192 and n.1). Reflexes of this same practice can be seen in the type of routine formalities displayed at the palace of the Persian kings, where it had become little more than a matter of theatricality and ceremonious pomp (A. Christensen, *L'Iran sous les Sassanides*, 2nd ed., Copenhagen 1944, 395–404). But it also was a custom well known among tribal leaders of the Scythian nomads: cf. e.g. A. Maskell, *Russian art and art objects in Russia* (London 1884) 56–7, where the domestic situation corresponds far more closely than any grand palace setting to what we are told by Greek sources about the arrangements in Pythagoras' own home (Diogenes Laertius, loc. cit.: "... they were only able to hear Pythagoras speaking, and were never allowed to see him until they had been tested and accepted; but from then on they were allowed inside his home, became a part of his household and were included in the number of people permitted to see him"). Here, as elsewhere, the Persian royal protocol doubtless had its ultimate origin in the much older steppe customs of central and northern Asia. And as for the other tradition about Pythagoras having a thigh made of gold, along with its implicit background in shamanic rituals of dismemberment followed by reconstruction: recent discoveries are making it increasingly clear that the heartland of such practices and rituals is Central Asia. See Chu Junjie in *Theses on Tibetology in China*, ed. Hu Tan (Beijing 1991) 133; V.A. Semyonov in *Tsentralnaya Aziya i Pribaykalye v drevosti*, ed. M.V. Konstantinov and A.D. Tsybiktarov (Ulan-Ude 2002) 88–92; J.V. Bellezza, *Zhang Zhung* (Vienna 2008) 556–7; above, note 21.

On the destruction of Pythagoras' original teaching center and network see note 21 above; and on the role assumed by Tarentum as the new center for Pythagoreanism, Burkert 116. For a general introduction to the Pythagorean culture of Tarentum cf. Kingsley, *Ancient philosophy* 133–65, 256–64: what is most striking about it is the constant overlapping of application and theory, of spirituality and science, mechanical ingenuity and philosophy, mysticism and military expertise, in an intricate pattern of interweaving almost incomprehensible today. This overlapping had implications which were not just remarkably practical, but deadly practical—including the design and creation, by people who were mystics as well as poets, of weaponry that in the West would hardly be improved on for hundreds or even thousands of years. And very much implicated in these activities was the extraordinary philosopher elected seven times as Tarentum's military commander: Archytas (cf. W. Burkert's comments in *Tra Sicilia e Magna Grecia*, ed. A.C. Cassio and D. Musti, Pisa 1989, 211; Kingsley, *Ancient philosophy* 144–58). Unfortunately academics are not often able to appreciate the extraordinary, in particular when it happens to be extraordinary because it combines the deepest spirituality with the most immediate practicality. And there is something very comical as well as sad about the way that recent scholarship has used every tool of seemingly rational argument at its disposal to create a portrait of Archytas in its own image by converting him into the quaint, bumbling prototype of a modern college professor: someone who, if he ever bothers putting his hand to anything, does so purely as an amateur and produces nothing more effective than playthings or toys (C.A. Huffman, *Archytas of Tarentum*, Cambridge 2005).

The figure of Archytas has a unique historical significance because—after the Golden Age of Athens had reached its culmination in the moment when Socrates was officially condemned to death—it was Archytas who, for better or worse, happened to host the disoriented and traumatized Plato in Italy. By way of returning this favor Plato would replicate the cosmological teachings he had received from Archytas' Sicilian and Italian disciples, not without many omissions and distortions, as the famous Platonic myths (Kingsley, *Ancient philosophy* 71–213); would go to considerable trouble to conceal his philosophical indebtedness to Archytas in other matters as well (L. Zhmud, *Phronesis* 43, 1998, 225–6 with n.48); and would spawn the criticism of Archytas, soon to be repeated and amplified by generation after generation of Platonists, that condemned him for corrupting the purity of abstract philosophical truth by daring to apply it in the everyday physical world (Kingsley, *Ancient philosophy* 157 n.36 with further references; note also L. Hodgkin's comments, *A history of mathematics*, Oxford 2005, 60–1 on the "Platonic propagandist viewpoint" of Plutarch's *Marcellus* 14–17). Considering the extent of western scholars' dependency on Plato for their legacy of uninhibited impracticality, it was predictable that they would instinctively take Plato's side on this issue and brood obsessively over the smallest details of what Plato might or might not have thought about Archytas: cf. e.g. G.E.R. Lloyd, *Phronesis* 35 (1990) 159–74, who trustingly but gullibly minimizes the extent to which the Platonic seventh letter (on its author see Kingsley, *Ancient philosophy* 343 n.24) is a creative rewriting of historical facts to help protect Plato against his many actual or potential critics, and Lloyd's *Principles and practices in ancient Greek and Chinese science* (Aldershot 2006) xii; Huffman 32–42; A. Barker, *Oxford studies in ancient philosophy* 31 (2006) 300–2. But there are far fewer people willing to pose the question of what exactly Archytas must have thought about Plato. After all, it was Plato in his naïveté who was responsible for the disastrous miscalculation of imagining that he had the ability to train a ruthless Sicilian tyrant to become a philosopher–king; when the tyrant responded by locking him up in prison and threatening his life it was Archytas who made all the necessary arrangements to have him rescued after Plato, as everyone would soon come to hear, had sent a message begging for help (L. Sprague de Camp, *The ancient engineers*, London 1963, 98; G.E.R. Lloyd and N. Sivin, *The way and the word*, New Haven, CT 2002, 90–1). The irony is that, if Archytas had not taken the practical steps needed to save him, there would have been no more Plato and no Platonic philosophers to condemn Archytas for his practicality. These are the strange moments and hidden paradoxes out of which history is made.

For the portrait of the Mongol from Tarentum see esp. E. Bielefeld, *Gnomon* 37 (1965) 215 (wisely noting how it "beweist erneut, wie eng die Welt damals bereits geworden war") and D. Metzler, *Porträt und Gesellschaft* (Münster 1971) 124–7; also K.R. Krierer in *Contacts between cultures*, ed. A. Harrak et al. (Lewiston, NY 1993) i 236–44. And as for the major fascination exerted on Pythagoreans in Archytas' Tarentum by Hyperboreans and Central Asia, along with some of the reasons behind it, see Wiesner 200–217.

This link between the Far East and the Tarentum of Archytas also helps us place other things in a far better perspective. For example, there is the extraordinary tradition about Archytas creating a wooden bird which was able to fly (Aulus Gellius, *Attic nights* 10.12.8–10; Favorinus fr. 93 Barigazzi). In trying to come to grips with this remarkable report, western scholars allowed their innate instinct for trivialization to spiral out of control and have ended up presenting Archytas' wooden bird as some elaborate toy that of course could never fly but was just an intricate after-dinner trick invented by him to impress and amuse his guests (so, most recently, Huffman 570–9. These fantastic explanations have been built on the feeblest of foundations by historians who fail even to note that the enigmatic rationalizations offered by Aulus Gellius, in terms of counterpoise and jets of air, were no more than speculative guesswork on his part. For his use of *scilicet*, "naturally" or "no doubt," to announce his own often dubious inferences and assumptions cf. e.g. *Attic nights* 6.20.6; and, for his clichéd attempt at a rationale, the material gathered by A. Deschard in *Recherches sur aura*, Leuven 2003, esp. 31–2). As for the profoundly mistaken idea that Pythagoreans were gentlemen who had nothing better to do with their time than to play entertaining games and invent fanciful toys see Kingsley, *Ancient philosophy* 157–8; even the rattle that Archytas is said to have designed had a very specific and practical purpose (Aristotle, *Politics* 1340b25–9). In reality we have no grounds for saying any more than that Archytas was an inventor of mechanical devices; that as a general he was keenly attentive to their military applications; and that he produced a wooden bird which, although capable of flying, was unable to take off again once it had landed (Favorinus fr. 93 Barigazzi; K. Luck-Huyse, *Der Traum vom Fliegen in der Antike*, Stuttgart 1997, 132).

All these details fall into place in the most interesting way as soon as we look at the larger picture—and see that Chinese inventors alive before Archytas not only became famous for solving the problem of how to produce a wooden bird which would fly, but also used this invention very specifically for military purposes. See e.g. Co-Ching Chu, *Geographical review* 5 (1918) 136–7; J. Needham, *Science and civilisation in China* iv/2 (Cambridge 1965) 573–4, 577–8; Hong-Sen Yan, *Reconstruction design of lost ancient Chinese machinery* (Dordrecht 2007) 270–3. On the methodological issues involved in positing the interconnectedness of such inventions across vast distances and different cultures, cf. J. Needham and Lu Gwei-Djen, *Trans-Pacific echoes and resonances* (Singapore 1985) 7–15; Mair, *Contact and exchange* 1–16. For the interrelations between ancient Chinese and Greek technologies of warfare see now Mair's comments in *The art of war: Sun Zi's military methods* (New York 2007) 42–6; and regarding Archytas' open acknowledgement of his debt as an engineer (not "architect" as mistranslated by Huffman 28–9, 256, 303) to the superior knowledge of non-Greeks cf. Diogenes Laertius 8.82 with P. Kingsley, *Journal of the Warburg and Courtauld Institutes* 57 (1994) 5 and nn.27–8, 7 n.42, *Lapis* 10 (1999) 65. For the role played by later Mongols in transmitting Chinese military technology, including flying devices, to the West see Needham, *Science and civilisation* iv/2 595–9 and v/7 (Cambridge 1986) 467,

570–7 with C.I. Beckwith's comments, *Journal of the Tibet Society* 7 (1987) 5.

28.

Avar connections from Europe to China: cf. e.g. V.H. Mair in *Proceedings of the sixteenth annual UCLA Indo-European conference*, ed. K. Jones-Bley et al. (Washington, DC 2005) 17 (Yu Hong) with J.A. Lerner, *Aspects of assimilation: the funerary practices and furnishings of Central Asians in China* (Sino-Platonic papers 168, Philadelphia 2005) 30 n.77, Lerner's Erratum to her p.5 n.6, and C.Z. Xie et al., *Proceedings of the Royal Society, Series B (Biological Sciences)* 274 (2007) 1597–1601; also S. Stark, *Ancient civilizations from Scythia to Siberia* 15 (2009). J. Weatherford's assertion (*Genghis Khan and the making of the modern world*, New York 2004, xix) that at the time of Genghis Khan's birth in the 12th century "no one in China had heard of Europe, and no one in Europe had heard of China, and, so far as is known, no person had made the journey from one to the other" could hardly be more wrong; see also above, note 27. The songs of the Avars: H.W. Haussig in *Geschichte Mittelasiens*, ed. K. Jettmar et al. (Leiden 1966) 112; S. Szádeczky-Kardoss in *The Cambridge history of early Inner Asia*, ed. D. Sinor (Cambridge 1990) 211, 228.

On the paradoxical combination of constancy and shiftingness in the name "Avar" itself see A. Alföldi, *Eurasia septentrionalis antiqua* 9 (1934) 290; W. Pohl, *Die Awaren* (Munich 1988) 38 (although Pohl tends to push this point too far in the name of modern ethnogenetic theory); and for the same situation with regard to Mongol tribes in general, W. Heissig, *The religions of Mongolia* (London 1980) 18. To P.B. Golden (*Encyclopaedia of Islam Three* 2009–3, Leiden 2009, 129–35) any direct connection between the Avars of Daghistan in the Caucasus, famous for becoming those Naqshbandi Sufis who with remarkable persistence resisted tsarist troops during the 19th century, and ancient Avars originating from the area now known as Mongolia "seems unlikely." But that there are no connections at all seems even more unlikely: cf. H.H. Howorth, *Journal of the Royal Asiatic Society* 21 (1889) 727–30; H.W. Haussig, *Byzantion* 23

(1953) 363–6 with n.346; H.W. Bailey, *Bulletin of the School of Oriental and African Studies* 42 (1979) 210; K. Czeglédy, *Archivum Eurasiae medii aevi* 3 (1983) 105. On the Naqshbandi Avars and their famous leader, Shamil, cf. H. Algar in *Naqshbandis*, ed. M. Gaborieau et al. (Istanbul 1990) 36; A. Bennigsen and C. Lemercier-Quelquejay, ibid. 441–2; M. Gammer, *Muslim resistance to the Tsar* (London 1992); *Russian–Muslim confrontation in the Caucasus*, ed. T. Sanders et al. (London 2004). And on the entry of this Avar Naqshbandi tradition into the modern world see J.S. Nielsen et al. in *Sufism in the West*, ed. J. Malik and J. Hinnells (Abingdon 2006) 103–114.

That the only history of the Avars is the one written by its enemies has become a routine observation in studies of them: cf. e.g. Pohl 1 and, for general comments on this same truth in its application to "barbarians" as a whole, G.G. Guzman, *Historian* 50 (1988) 558–9. On the astonishment expressed by Europeans at the Avars' miraculous generosity and kindness, especially in feeding strangers, see D.A. Tirr's summary, *Acta archaeologica Academiae Scientiarum Hungaricae* 28 (1976) 111–12. Note also the dramatic stories of warmth and hospitality shown to hostages by the supposedly barbarous Daghistani Avars under Shamil, which shocked the Russian media and intelligentsia (S. Layton, *Central Asian survey* 23, 2004, 183–203). There is an important cultural factor lying at the root of these phenomena that has been sadly neglected—the strong value attached in "barbarian," and especially Mongol, tradition to feeding enemies and strangers. Cf. Niẓām ad-Dīn Awliyāʾ, *Morals for the heart*, trans. B.B. Lawrence (Mahwah 1992) 99–100; D. DeWeese in *History and historiography of post-Mongol Central Asia and the Middle East: studies in honor of John E. Woods*, ed. J. Pfeiffer and S.A. Quinn (Wiesbaden 2006) 28–30.

### 29.

A few of the more surprising ways in which Mongols embodied ethical principles quite distinct from the corrupt values, and often cruel practices, of their supposedly civilized enemies are covered by J. Weatherford, *Genghis Khan and the making of the modern world* (New York 2004). For Genghis Khan's deliberate refusal to take advantage of opportunities which would allow him to promote a favorable image of himself, and his insistence on appearing in the worst possible light, see ibid. 114. A vivid, not to mention moving, account of one influential Muslim's response to the Mongol devastation is offered by ʿAṭāʾ Malik Juvaynī, *Genghis Khan: the history of the world–conqueror*, trans. J.A. Boyle (2ⁿᵈ ed., Seattle 1997) 104.

For Sufis' perceptions of Genghis Khan see especially the material assembled and discussed by D. DeWeese in *History and historiography of post-Mongol Central Asia and the Middle East: studies in honor of John E. Woods*, ed. J. Pfeiffer and S.A. Quinn (Wiesbaden 2006) 23–60; and cf. also L. Lewisohn, *Beyond faith and infidelity* (Richmond, Surrey 1995) 57–8, M. Biran, *Chinggis Khan* (Oxford 2007) 112–14, J. Elverskog, *Buddhism and Islam on the Silk Road* (Philadelphia 2010) 201. On the "Pole" see H. Corbin, *The man of light in Iranian Sufism* (Boulder 1978); P. Kingsley, *Ancient philosophy, mystery and magic* (Oxford 1995) 380–1 with note 20 above; Nūr ad-Dīn ʿAbd ar-Raḥmān Jāmī, *Fragrant breezes of intimate friendship*, trans. M. Holland (Fort Lauderdale 2010). For Khidr cf. *Qurʾān* 18:60–82; P. Franke, *Begegnung mit Khidr* (Beirut 2000); T.M. van Lint in *Redefining Christian identity: cultural interaction in the Middle East since the rise of Islam*, ed. J.J. van Ginkel (Leuven 2005) 361–78. Sufi visions of Genghis Khan's army as not only embodying the wrath of God but also being guided invisibly by spiritual beings (DeWeese 34–42, 51–2) bear a striking similarity to visions of the great Mahākāla riding, thanks to Tibetan Buddhist rituals, in the sky above the army of Kublai Khan as it swept into China (E. Sperling in *Imagining Tibet*, ed. T. Dodin and H. Räther, Boston 2001, 320). And it should be added that the issue of how Sufis came to perceive the invading armies of Genghis Khan is, in the last resort, inseparable from the issue of the very close links between Central Asian Sufism and shamanism. On those links see e.g. M.F. Köprülü, *Influence du chamanisme turco-mongol sur les ordres mystiques musulmans* (Istanbul 1929) and *Islam in Anatolia after the Turkish invasion* (Salt Lake City 1993); H.S. Nyberg, *Die Religionen des alten Iran* (Leipzig 1938) 167, 173–4; I. Mélikoff, *Turcica* 20 (1988) 7–18; V.N Basilov, *Diogenes* 158 (1992) 16–17; D. DeWeese's study,

*Islamization and native religion in the Golden Horde* (University Park, PA 1994); T. Zarcone in *La politique des esprits*, ed. D. Aigle et al. (Nanterre 2000) 383–96 (which is a far more satisfactory analysis than R. Amitai-Preiss' remarkably superficial discussion in *Journal of the economic and social history of the Orient* 42, 1999, 38–42) and *Kyoto bulletin of Islamic area studies* 1 (2007) 52–61; A. Rozwadowski in *The archaeology of shamanism*, ed. N.S. Price (London 2001) 72; J.P. Berkey, *The formation of Islam* (Cambridge 2003) 245–6; B. Sidikov in *Shamanism*, ed. M.N. Walter and E.J. Neumann-Fridman (Santa Barbara 2004) i 238–42.

For the comparison of Genghis Khan's army to a wildfire see also B. Prakash, *International review of history and political science* 1 (1964) 93: "In this time of gloom and despair, bribery and corruption, exaction and exploitation, the Mongols came like a wildfire to consume and remove the pernicious growths and prepare the field for a new crop." On the religious openness and tolerance of the Mongols cf. J.G. Bennett, *The masters of wisdom* (London 1977) 145, 150; T. Haining, *Asian affairs* 17 (1986) 26–7; J.-P. Roux, *Revue de l'histoire des religions* 203 (1986) 131–68; Lewisohn 62–4, 82–92, 294; M.T. Kapstein, *The Tibetan assimilation of Buddhism* (New York 2000) 99; Weatherford 58, 69, 104, 173–4, 219–20, 233–6; J. Elverskog, *Our great Qing* (Honolulu 2006) 101–4 and in *The Mongolia–Tibet interface*, ed. U.E. Bulag and H.G.M. Diemberger (Leiden 2007) 59–80; Biran 67–8. This openness is just a little too much for many western commentators, who feel duty-bound to warn their readers that they need to treat it with utmost cynicism. We are assured that in the eyes of Mongols themselves it was purely "pragmatic" or politically motivated, as opposed to genuinely "mystical" (cf. e.g. Lewisohn 88, misquoting Roux, and other examples of modern commentaries in C.P. Atwood, *International history review* 26, 2004, 237–56; P. Jackson in *Mongols, Turks and others*, ed. R. Amitai and M. Biran, Leiden 2004, 253–78). There are writers so determined to deny the Mongols any credit or genuine originality for anything that they are even willing to invert realities by describing "the tolerance of the Mongols" as being "modelled on the religious pluralism of Sufism" (L. Lewisohn in *The heritage of Sufism* iii, ed. Lewisohn and D. Morgan, Oxford 1999, 69; for some cautions about the belief that Sufis outside of certain specific circles were particularly tolerant in religious matters see T. Zarcone's comments, *The Tibet journal* 20/3, 1995, 106–7, while on the general subject of religious tolerance in India aside from the influence exerted by the Moghuls cf. Roux 134). And one of the most influential modern experts on the Mongols insists, with a moral tone strongly reminiscent of Christian writers in the Middle Ages, that their tolerance was just a thing of the moment and had no spine to it at all ("religious belief as such seems to have sat rather lightly on the Mongols ... The Mongols' lack of religious fervour is well demonstrated in one of their most lauded characteristics, their firm policy of religious tolerance ... Toleration there certainly was, but it was determined not so much by high-mindedness as by indifference ...": D. Morgan, *The Mongols*, 2nd ed., Oxford 2007, 37–8). But why pragmatism and mysticism should have become polar opposites is among the greatest mysteries and wonders of the modern western world. It was no small practical achievement for the Mongol Khans to transform into a major institution the long-standing Central Asian custom (Jackson 253) of convening formal gatherings made up of representatives from different religions so they could openly discuss their beliefs on an equal footing instead of just killing each other. These conferences were carried outward with the help of the Mongols from Central Asia into China and India, Iran and Anatolia (Roux 146–51). Their format as well as the spirit behind them helped sow the seeds in a few receptive individuals of the immediate experience that there is a greater reality lying beyond the relativity of religious tenets and dogmas. This in turn created an environment which would exert a profound influence on some of the greatest Persian Sufis (Lewisohn 63–4, 82–92), on rare beacons of religious tolerance in the earlier history of Tibetan Buddhism such as Karma Pakshi (Kapstein 97–106, 244 n.81; above, note 24), and indirectly even on a number of broad-minded Christians. Beyond such considerations, though, is the overarching reality that religious tolerance among the Mongols was originally and essentially a symptom not of weakness but of great strength—of the shamanic awareness that the sacred is manifest everywhere, in everything, and that nothing could be more absurd than to imagine the divine in all its vastness can be confined to just one book or building or institution (Haining 26; Roux 158–9; Weatherford 6).

This all-inclusiveness was by its very nature much more pragmatic, far more tangible and down-to-earth, than anybody would normally expect. It would be extremely reasonable to assume that during what later came to be known as the lowest point in Genghis Khan's life as a warrior, when he was on the run and had been abandoned almost alone with just a handful of supporters beside a muddy lake in the wildest and remotest regions of Mongolia, those few people who stood by him must all have been followers of the native shamanic religion like he was. But nothing could be further from the truth. They included Muslims and Buddhists and Christians, joined to each other in a shared sense of service and commitment, all ready to live and die together (Atwood 244; Weatherford 57–8).

This simple transcendence of religious differences among the Mongols was a prospect that, even if only on an unconscious level, terrified many of their enemies almost as much as all the death and destruction. And the way things had begun for Genghis Khan was how they would continue. Accounts describe Islamic Sufis as holding positions of power in his immediate circle (Niẓām ad-Dīn Awliyā', *Morals for the heart*, trans. B.B. Lawrence, Mahwah 1992, 99; DeWeese in *History and historiography of post-Mongol Central Asia* 28–30). And when the Mongol army reached as far into Europe as it ever would, to the forests outside of Vienna, the Christian troops were scared out of their senses when they captured a Mongol scout who turned out to be a well-educated English nobleman. Before they killed him they managed to find out that, after many adventures, he had been forced into exile and had discovered a very welcoming home among the Mongols (Haining 22, Weatherford 157–8: on the Mongol empire as safe haven for exiles or refugees see Roux 139).

But of course there is more to this matter than just a factual misunderstanding regarding the one, specific topic of religious tolerance. A few historians are gradually starting to piece together the fascinating story about the many psychological strategies invented by civilized people around the world for maintaining a sense of racial, moral, intellectual and spiritual superiority over the Mongols. And wherever these strategies find expression, they are always predictably similar. The nomadic Mongol is an inferior creature: just an animal waiting to be tamed and trained, domesticated, prodded by its cultured masters into settling down and converting to whatever religion those masters happen to belong to (cf. esp. K. Kollmar-Paulenz's discussion in *Images of Tibet in the 19th and 20th centuries*, ed. M. Esposito, Paris 2008, ii 707–24; also Elverskog in *The Mongolia–Tibet interface* 59–80). This has come to mean that we in the West project our own inner darkness onto the Mongols, just as we have learned to project our internal spiritual longing onto Tibet (for the deceptiveness of such projections see e.g. P.N. Jones' comments, *Respect for the ancestors*, Boulder 2005, 204). By and large even the most apparently impartial and learned western scholars are finding it almost impossible to come out untouched from underneath all the centuries of this very human prejudice and animosity. And the identical basic dynamics are present, regardless of any Buddhist idealism, in the almost ineradicable Tibetan assumption of superiority to the Mongols—"who, because of their inherent cultural and religious inferiority, could never be equal to Tibetans" (Kollmar-Paulenz 709–10). On one hand, the Dalai Lamas soon learned how to erase very systematically any signs of the role played by Mongols in shaping Tibetan Buddhism (cf. e.g. J. Powers, *Introduction to Tibetan Buddhism*, 2nd ed., Ithaca, NY 2007, 168; for the resulting fantasies as recounted by T. Laird, *The story of Tibet*, New York 2006, 138–47 see note 24 above). On the other hand, the standard historical view still widely promoted is that the Mongol barbarians were the ones who stood to gain from Tibet because in their primitive eyes "Tibetan culture was advanced and attractive, with much to covet" (Laird 139). But this apparently innocent idea of Mongols "coveting" Tibetan civilization conceals a great deal more than it reveals. At the root of what was so scaring to civilized people in Asia as well as Europe about the Mongols was not only the impending threat of physical death and destruction, or the threat they posed to religious monopolies and exclusivities, but also an extremely uncomfortable awareness that at the time of their greatest power the Mongols happened to care very little for the trappings of so-called culture. Genghis Khan himself conquered hundreds of cities but hardly ever, unless he felt compelled to do so for a very specific reason, even set foot in any of them; he was happiest withdrawing as quickly as possible back into the countryside. And when centuries later Altan Khan came right up to Beijing and had the capital city in the palm of his hand he withdrew, to the amazement of the terrified Chinese, because he was not interested in more power or land: all he wanted was cooperation, just treatment for his people and fair trade. We can either write history as a way of placing our own values and prejudices at the center of every picture, or we can choose to allow for what sometimes is referred to as the "nomadic alternative"—a term politely coined by some recent researchers to celebrate their growing realization that nomadic people might have had some sound reasons for wanting to live their own life in their own way (cf. e.g. B. Genito in *Proceedings of the 5th conference of the Societas Iranologica Europæa* i, ed. A. Panaino and A. Piras, Milan 2006, 75–100).

For the new life brought by Mongols—their sowing of entirely fresh possibilities; their cross-fertilization of cultures; the realities of international law and science, medicine and art, travel and trade that they introduced into the world alongside everything else—see e.g. G.G. Guzman, *Historian* 50 (1988) 566–70, as well as the two studies by Weatherford and Biran. And, as it always manages to do, life shows itself in the most paradoxical and unexpected ways. Nowadays riding horses in Mongolia and spending time with local shamans is being hailed as the latest method of treatment for childhood autism (R. Isaacson, *The horse boy*, New York 2009): a peculiar irony considering how in the mid-nineteenth century a British doctor, confronted with what would come to be known as Down syndrome, had originally given birth to the term "Mongolism" as a medical label for the "large number of congenital idiots" who due to their retarded state "are typical Mongols" (J.L.H. Down, *Clinical lectures & reports by the medical & surgical staff of the London Hospital* 3, 1866, 259–62; a century later, official steps were taken to find a replacement for the term because of its racial implications). But the profoundest, and most timeless, expression of civilized people's need for what only barbarians can offer remains Konstantinos Kavafis' nineteenth-century poem *Waiting for the barbarians*.

## 30.

The particular tradition about the bundle of five arrows already features, very prominently, almost at the start of the oldest surviving Mongol text: "Alan the Fair assembled her five sons together. She seated them all in a row, gave them each the shaft of an arrow and said to them: 'Break it!' A single arrow shaft, it took no great strength to break it, and each of them broke it and tossed it away. Then she bound together five shafts in a bundle, and giving the bundle to each in his turn, said to each of them: 'Break it!' Each of the brothers held the five bound together and no one could break them. ... Then Alan the Fair spoke to her five sons and gave them this advice: 'You five were all born from one womb. If, like the five single arrows that you held you separate yourselves, each going alone, then each of you can be broken by anyone. If you are drawn together by a singular purpose bound like the five shafts in a bundle how can anyone break you?'" (*The secret history of the Mongols* §§19–22, trans. P. Kahn and F.W. Cleaves, 2nd ed., Boston 1998, 5–6; on the episode see W. Hung's comments, *Harvard journal of Asiatic studies* 14, 1951, 486–7). And it recurs, down to the smallest details, in the tradition about how Hiawatha came to establish the Great Law of Peace which gave rise to the Iroquois Confederacy of the five tribes: "He was shown a single arrow—and how easily it could be snapped in two. Then he was shown a vision of five arrows banded together—they could not be broken. Hiawatha then summoned a great council of the five New York tribes" (A.G. Adams, *The Catskills*, New York 1990, 75; cf. R.P. Carlisle and J.G. Golson, *Native America from prehistory to first contact*, Santa Barbara 2007, 103). Or as this understanding would be formalized: "Five arrows shall be bound together very strong and each arrow shall represent one nation. As the five arrows are strongly bound this shall symbolize the complete union of the nations. Thus are the Five

Nations united completely and enfolded together, united into one head, one body and one mind. Therefore they shall labor, legislate and council together for the interest of future generations" (A.C. Parker, *The constitution of the five nations* = *New York State Museum bulletin* 184, Albany 1916, 11, 45, 101–2; cf. *Concerning the League: the Iroquois League tradition as dictated in Onondaga by John Arthur Gibson*, ed. H. Woodbury, Winnipeg 1992, 299–307).

The exact correspondences between these Mongol and Iroquois traditions are most certainly no coincidence. For the migrations of women and men from Mongolia and Siberia, across the Pacific, to become the Native Americans see note 25 above. For the transmission of lore from the Mongols specifically to the Iroquois, cf. e.g. W.B. Gibbon, *Journal of American folklore* 77/305 (1964) 236–50 and 85/337 (1972) 236–47; note Kara Dawne Zemel's meaningful observations in *The eastern door* 13/32 (September 3, 2004) 17; and see esp. J.A. Stewart in *The 8ᵗʰ international congress of Mongolists being convened under the patronage of N. Bagabandi* (Ulaanbaatar 2002) 173–4.

A symbolic grouping of five arrows is already mentioned in ancient Greek literature, by the father of western history, as being very characteristically Scythian: see Herodotus, *Histories* 4.131 (*oistous pente*) and, for the links between Scythian traditions as reported by Greeks and traditions known from Mongolia, note 2 above. When discussing other details in this passage of Herodotus Stephanie West wisely cites parallels from Mongolia as well as Tibet, even referring for one specific matter to *The secret history of the Mongols*, and has some good things to say about the uses of coded language and symbolism by Asiatic nomads as forms of communication (*Journal of Hellenic studies* 108, 1988, 207–11). But she overlooks the crucial fact that the motif of five arrows, neither more nor less, also occurs in *The secret history*. This automatically invalidates her—otherwise very implausible—suggestion that the alternative account of the Scythian episode as provided by Clement of Alexandria, which mentions just a single arrow instead of five (*Stromata* 5.8.44.2–4, 355.19–26 Stählin), is more accurate and authentic than the one in Herodotus. On the symbolic significance that came to be attributed to a bundle of five arrows in Tibetan

Buddhism see R. Beer, *The encyclopedia of Tibetan symbols and motifs* (Boston 1999) 276. It also will be noted that, even when the tale about the unbreakable bundle lost its link with the number five after arriving in Europe, the story still retained its Scythian associations (L. Gibbs, *Aesop's fables*, Oxford 2002, 227–8).

For the Iroquois bundle of arrows and the transmission of its symbolism into the imagery on the Great Seal of the United States (where eventually it became thirteen arrows, corresponding to the number of the original states) see e.g. J. and D.G. Campbell, *Journal of Cherokee studies* 6 (1981) 93; B.E. Johansen and B.A. Mann, *Encyclopedia of the Haudenosaunee* (Westport, CT 2000) 35; L.J. Favor, *The Iroquois constitution* (New York 2003) 44; R. Wright, *Stolen continents* (2nd ed., New York 2005) 116. For the profound influence exerted by Iroquois symbolism and imagery on Benjamin Franklin, as well as his conscious indebtedness to it, see S. Kalter, *Benjamin Franklin, Pennsylvania and the First Nations* (Champaign 2006) 89 with 120 n.2. And regarding the general influence of the Iroquois system, as well as of individual Iroquois, on the forming of the United States Constitution see J. Kleiner, *Case and comment* 77/4 (July–August 1972) 5; Campbell and Campbell 92–3; C.L. Bagley and J.A. Ruckman, *American Indian culture and research journal* 7/2 (1983) 53–72; J. Weatherford, *Indian givers* (New York 1988) 133–50; B.E. Johansen, *Ethnohistory* 37 (1990) 279–90; D.A. Grinde and B.E. Johansen, *William and Mary quarterly* 53 (1996) 621–36; J. Needleman, *The American soul* (New York 2002) 197–203 with 368 n.92; Wright 116; and cf. also the judicious comments in Kalter 23–9.

On what this tells us about the sophistication of "pre-contact" Native American culture, and the Iroquois League in particular, see e.g. Parker 11 ("… absolute unanimity was the law and required for the passage of any question. Provisions to break speedily any deadlock were provided. All the work of the council was done without an executive head … civil chiefs were nominated by certain noble women in whose families the titles were hereditary; the nominations were confirmed by popular councils both of men and of women and finally by the confederate council. Women thus had great power for not only could they nominate their rulers but also depose them for incompetency in office. Here, then, we find the right of popular nomination, the right of recall and of woman suffrage, all flourishing in the old America of the Red Man and centuries before it became the clamor of the new America of the white invader. Who now shall call Indians and Iroquois savages!"); cf. also L.H. Morgan, *League of the Ho-dé-no-sau-nee* (Rochester, NY 1851), Wright 117–21.

The subtle and overt influence exerted by the Iroquois on the emerging United States extended far beyond the level of imagery or symbolism, embracing the deepest aspects of life and liberty and democracy. For some fine comments on these deeper dimensions, and on the necessary process of compromise that led the Founding Fathers towards diluting the purity of Native practices so as to accommodate the ingrained British and European craving to manipulate and exploit other humans, see C.C. Mann, *1491* (New York 2006) 369–78.

Naturally there are some American politicians and historians who insist on denying any connection between Native Americans and the forming of the United States, just as there are some Native Americans who deny any connection between themselves and Asia—and some Tibetan Buddhists who deny that their beliefs and practices ever had any connection with indigenous shamans. Human nature is sadly, but also very beautifully, consistent. And there is a wonderfully elegant symmetry in the formal announcement made by a prominent American classical scholar when she declares that of course the Iroquois played no more of a part in the evolution of the United States Constitution than non-Greek barbarians played in "the invention of what we now call philosophy" (Mary Lefkowitz, *Wall Street journal*, March 24, 1997, A.16).

## 31.

On the Great Taboo, its historical background and its aftermath, see D.A. DeWeese, *Islamization and native religion in the Golden Horde* (University Park, PA 1994) 179–203; J. Weatherford, *Genghis Khan and the making of the modern world* (New York 2004) xxi–xxii, xxvlll-xxxiii. Regarding the present state of affairs cf. M. Kohn, *Mongolia* (5th ed., Footscray 2008) 172.

For Genghis Khan and ecstasy see the detailed description in Minhāj ad-Dīn Jūzjānī, *Ṭabaqāt-i Nāṣirī*, trans. H.G. Raverty (London 1881) ii 1077–8; J.A. Boyle, *Folklore* 83 (1972) 181. Note also D. Ermakov's comments both on Genghis Khan as ecstatic spiritual leader and on the phenomenon of ecstatic warfare among Mongols: *Bo and Bön* (Kathmandu 2008) 86–8. For the ecstasies of Shamil, the Naqshbandi Avar leader (above, note 28), cf. P.B. Golden, *International journal of Middle East studies* 27 (1995) 522.

It of course is normal practice among most modern intellectuals to complain about "all the obfuscation of ecstasy" that surrounds the subject of shamanism (C. Humphrey in *Shamanism, history and the state*, ed. N. Thomas and Humphrey, Ann Arbor 1994, 204)—implying that the messy subject of ecstasy should not be allowed to complicate the approach to shamanism as a purely social and political phenomenon. In much the same way, people excited by the modern resurgence of curiosity about ancient Greek philosophy as a "spiritual" phenomenon fail to notice that the author most responsible for this resurgent interest is extremely careful to present the spirituality of the Greek philosophers as something always subjected to "a rigorous need for rational control" and devoid of any ecstasy—even if this involves systematically falsifying the evidence (P. Hadot, *What is ancient philosophy?*, Cambridge, MA 2002, 180–6; for a sound criticism of Hadot and his methods see P. Gignoux, *Man and cosmos in ancient Iran*, Rome 2001, 84–5; and for the case of Empedocles, so poorly handled by Hadot, cf. P. Kingsley, *Ancient philosophy* 22, 2002, 399–404 and *Reality*, Inverness, CA 2003, 438–41). But the truth, independent of intellectual fashions, is that the state of ecstasy is always the key; and everything else is the obfuscation.

On the ecstasies not only of Abaris but also of Aristeas, who traveled out east from Greece towards Central Asia and is related to Abaris in a number of ways, see notes 2 and 15 above. For Pythagoras and ecstasy see the scholia to Homer's *Odyssey* 1.371 (i 64.12–13 Dindorf) = H. Thesleff, *The Pythagorean texts of the*

*Hellenistic period* (Åbo 1965) 172.6–7; W. Burkert, *Lore and science in ancient Pythagoreanism* (Cambridge, MA 1972) 357; P. Kingsley, *In the dark places of wisdom* (Inverness, CA 1999) 129–31. For the ecstatic roots of western logic, science and healing see Kingsley, *Dark places* and *Reality*.

## 32.

There are many passages where Plato, very clearly following older sources, articulates the ancient understanding about the end of civilizations and times of global extinction. Just to quote one of them, from the last book he wrote before he died: "Many times it has happened that humans have been wiped out by cataclysms and plagues and many other kinds of disasters. But, each time, a tiny portion of the human race managed to survive. Let's just consider one of the many different forms of devastation that have occurred: the case of a 'cataclysm' or deluge. Those few who managed to escape annihilation probably lived way up in the mountains—tiny embers of the human race kept alive somewhere high in the peaks and saved from complete extinction. But as for the cities and centers of civilization down in the plains and close to the sea, we can assume they were totally annihilated. All the tools and instruments and machinery were destroyed. Even the slightest trace of all the valuable arts and skills and technologies that had taken so much care and effort to discover simply vanished because, if everything stayed the whole time just the same as it is now, how could anything new have ever been invented? So this is what was left of human experience at the time of the devastation—terrifying, infinite desolation; enormous wastes of land without limit; almost all living creatures made utterly extinct" (*Laws* 677a–e, abbreviated).

To a well-known contemporary cosmologist called Brian Swimme we owe not only a modern and supposedly scientific worldview which is more naïve and simplistic than many ancient Greek cosmologies, but also announcements such as these: "Every now and then, the Earth goes through a die-off of the diversity of life ... We didn't know about this two hundred years ago; we didn't have the slightest idea that the Earth did this. Now we've discovered that around every hundred million years, the Earth went through these amazing cataclysms ... There was no awareness of this any previous time in human history. You look through the Vedas, you look in the Bible—it's nowhere ... The point is that we haven't been prepared to understand what an extinction event is. We've had all these great teachers. We've had tremendously intelligent people, going back through time, but you can look, for example, through all the *sutras* or Plato's dialogues, and they never talk about an extinction. As a matter of fact, I don't think that Plato or the Buddha were even capable of imagining an extinction. First of all, at that time we weren't aware of evolution. We weren't aware of the whole process, so the idea of extinction didn't make sense" (*What is enlightenment?* 19, Spring–Summer 2001, 38–9). Such a striking set of statements—ironically characterized by the very same sense of superiority and self-importance which helped to create our modern environmental catastrophe—is bound to raise a question about what, aside from all the rhetoric, evolution really is. And if our modern authorities understand so little about the past, it seems highly uncertain how reliable they could be as guides into the future.


**33.**

For the legend of the impenetrable mountains among early Mongols see e.g. P.A. Boodberg, *Harvard journal of Asiatic studies* 1 (1936) 180–1 and 3 (1938) 241; D. Sinor in *Folklorica: Festschrift for Felix J. Oinas*, ed. E.V. Zygas and P. Voorheis (Bloomington 1982) 246–8; D. Ermakov, *Bo and Bön* (Kathmandu 2008) 80. In Tibetan Bön tradition: G. Coleman, *A handbook of Tibetan culture* (London 1993) 13; Tenzin Wangyal, *Wonders of the natural mind* (Ithaca, NY 2000) 43; Ermakov 363–4. On the Rigvedic myth of the archer god who shoots his arrow through the impenetrable mountains, and its origin in ancient non-Aryan traditions of magic and sorcery, see F.B.J. Kuiper, *Aryans in the Rigveda* (Amsterdam 1991) 16–18.

The doubts expressed by S.W. Jamison (*Classical antiquity* 18, 1999, 266 n.105) about Kuiper's conclusions are quite unwarranted: cf. M. Witzel in F.B.J. Kuiper, *Selected writings on Indian linguistics and philology* (Amsterdam 1997) xx with n.45.

As soon as these Central Asian legends reached the eastern edges of Europe via the ancient Scythians, they started being subjected to a very ironic but also predictable inversion of their original sense—so that eventually the Mongols breaking through the mountains would come to be viewed no longer as marking the beginning of civilization but as announcing its apocalyptic end. For some general historical comments see P.G. Bietenholz, *Historia and fabula* (Leiden 1994) 121–37. And as a specific example cf. Matthew Paris' *Greater chronicles* for the year 1240 = *Matthaei Parisiensis chronica majora*, ed. H.R. Luard, iv (London 1877) 76: *ne mortalium gaudia continuentur, ne sine lamentis mundana laetitia diu celebretur, eodem anno plebs Sathanae detestanda, Tartarorum scilicet exercitus infinitus, a regione sua montibus circumvallata prorupit; et saxorum immeabilium soliditate penetrata, exeuntes ad instar daemonum solutorum a tartaro, ut bene Tartari, quasi tartarei, nuncupentur, scatebant* (for Matthew's identification here of Tartars with Tartarus, see Bietenholz 133 n.35; J.M. Hobson, *The eastern origins of western civilization*, Cambridge 2004, 45–6). As for the wise wolf, it was of course reduced to a cunning fox (C. Burnett and P. Gautier Dalché, *Viator* 22, 1991, 162).

Persian Sufis, on the other hand, were able to preserve the theme of the impenetrable mountains faithfully in its original sense. Cf. *The mystical and visionary treatises of Shihabuddin Yahya Suhrawardi*, trans. W.M. Thackston (London 1982) 37, 43 (reprinted as *The philosophical allegories and mystical treatises*, Costa Mesa 1999, 23, 32) = Shihâboddîn Yahyâ Sohravardî, *L'Archange empourpré*, trans. H. Corbin (Paris 1976) 204, 212.

My special thanks to
Walter Burkert, Johan Elverskog, Laura Gemelli Marciano,
Peter Golden, Lobsang Lhalungpa, Ani Jinpa Lhamo,
Victor Mair, Antonia Mills, Sarangerel Odigan, Lin Ying,
and to everyone from around the world who
helped bring this book into being

PETER KINGSLEY works with the sacred
tradition that gave birth to the western world. His
revolutionary understanding of the history as well
as the destiny of western civilization has changed
many people on the deepest level — transforming
their awareness not only of who they are but also
of their purpose in the modern world. Recognized
internationally for his groundbreaking work, he is
the recipient of numerous academic awards and
honors.

For further information visit
www.peterkingsley.org

"This is a small book. You can read it in an hour. I suggest that you read it several times and really get the golden idea at its core. Then bring that idea to everything you do—every decision, every choice, every plan, every interpretation. Live by an entirely different guidance. Walk like you've never walked before."

— THOMAS MOORE, author of *Care of the Soul*
and *The Re-enchantment of Everyday Life*